RECOGNIZING THE POWER OF YOUR VOICE

TERMS, WORDS, AND CONCEPTS THAT ALL PATIENTS SHOULD KNOW

SANDRA L. WASHINGTON

Foreword by Carolyn P. Coleman MHSA, RN, BSN

www.khpublishers.com

FOREWORD

Encouraging patients to speak up for themselves and maximize their engagement with their healthcare providers is not a mere theory. It's a critical requirement for the effectiveness of their health and well-being. Patients must speak up about their healthcare needs and challenges to better understand their and their providers' roles and responsibilities.

As a registered nurse for 38 years with a varied background in critical care nursing and case management, I advocate for my patients and educate them regarding their health issues, care and remediation processes, healthcare appointments, and treatment plans. I encourage them to write down their cares and concerns so that all their questions can be answered. This gives them greater control over managing their healthcare and holding their providers more accountable.

Full disclosure and in the spirit of transparency, I met Sandra Washington during a virtual book fair where she set the stage for her blueprint for documenting what every patient and their family needs to keep track of and manage their healthcare and well-being. She spoke about the *Personal Health Journal, and Planner,* which she created as her attempt to provide a foundation for patients to start with. I was impressed and immediately connected to her message.

In her latest work, *Recognizing the Power of Your Voice: Terms, Words, and Concepts That All Patients* Should Know, Sandra takes us on a personal journey through her bout with COVID-19. The closeness and connection you will feel as you follow her diary entries will draw you into what she experienced during her tribulation. You will feel her anger, disappointment, and displeasure with her healthcare providers. You will also feel the power in her voice as she advocated for herself so she could receive the healthcare she deserved.

Sandra not only dealt with the challenges riddled throughout the healthcare system, she understands how rampant these challenges are for those in marginalized communities. Advocating for yourself and your health could mean the difference between life and death. Sandra encourages patients to use their voices to ask questions until they receive a meaningful answer and to inform their healthcare providers of their concerns. This approach, she believes, will demonstrate that you, as a patient or the loved one of a patient, are engaged in your or their healthcare. Our voices need to be heard when we speak about our health and healthcare needs.

Sandra's journey is our journey. We all know someone from a marginalized community. Whether you are a patient care advocate, caregiver, patient, or future patient, this book can help you on your healthcare journey.

...In all your getting get understanding Proverbs 4:7 (KJV)

-Carolyn P. Coleman MHSA, RN BSN

NOTE FROM THE AUTHOR

The thought process behind the writing of this book was to use my experience as a Patient Advocate and show how my expertise helped me through one life-threatening health challenge I faced, COVID-19. I used that as a backdrop to point out the importance of a patient (specifically a patient labeled as marginalized) to advocate for optimal healthcare.

I've added my own personal experience on the days before, during, and after my time as a COVID-19 patient because I wanted each reader to know the personal advocacy struggles that I endured and how I had to find the strength to continuously campaign for my best health outcomes.

In writing this book, using a series of notes and thoughts from my diary, I hope each person who reads this book will be able to learn from my experience and about the advocacy tools, policies, and procedures that a Board-Certified

Patient Advocate should use to fight for your healthcare.

My intent and goal are to set in action a world where all patients are empowered to recognize, advocate for, and understand the importance of owning their healthcare.

PREFACE

January 20, 2020, was the beginning of a tumultuous period in the United States. It was on this day that a report regarding the Sars-Cov2/Novel Coronavirus, more commonly referred to as COVID-19, and its emerging presence in the United States was reported. Shortly afterward, in February 2020, the first reported death of a United States citizen tied directly to this deadly virus was reported. The reporting of the first person's death due to the COVID-19 virus was followed by an onslaught of attention-grabbing televised media reports and factual and fictitious social media postings. Since this was a novel virus, there was no predecessor from which data could be drawn, and the authorities were unclear on what or how to react to the changes that would be forthcoming. As the virus, which became known as a "Pandemic," continued to emerge, the consistent media hype had a definite impact on placing fear about the unknown into the minds of the American people.

As the constant press briefings from political leaders took their course, there was a barrage of information regarding the signs and symptoms of exposure to the 2019 novel Coronavirus. Data began to be publicized and caused mass hysteria among the public. The panic exacerbated the decline of access to necessities like toilet paper, disinfectant products, and paper towels. Supermarkets and grocery stores everywhere began to witness how quickly these items flew off store shelves. Clinical team members, including doctors and nurses, began to verbalize the symptoms appearing in people who had tested positive for the virus. Simultaneously, political leaders started sharing graphing maps showing the number of people who tested positive for the virus per state, city, and region. It was the start of a bubble ready to burst.

Reports juxtaposing the similarities and differences between the 1918 Spanish Flu, the 1957 Asian Flu, the 1968 Hong Kong Flu, HIV, SARS, the 2009 Swine Flu, 2012 MERS, and EBOLA were now being published by historians. I opine that focus was given to these prior pandemics to remove the fear of unsettlement that was beginning to take shape with the consistent media coverage of the COVID-19 virus. The fact remained that we were now faced with another deadly Pandemic. This pandemic would once again shine a light on the inequalities of social and economic impact that occur in marginalized communities whenever a global health crisis arises and which directly affected me, my family, and my loved ones.

The World Health Organization (WHO) describes a Pandemic as an epidemic (a disease that affects a large group of people that inhabit a community, population, or region) that occurs worldwide or over a vast area, one which crosses international boundaries with the potential of affecting a large group of people. It was clear that a pandemic had now reached the United States.

INTRODUCTION

As a Black woman who has studied and practicedhealthcare policy and procedures for over thirty years, I have witnessed the inequities in healthcare for brown and Black patients over the age of twenty-six—particularly women who often take the lead role in ensuring that their family's healthcare needs are met. The challenge for this specific group of patients is not that they do not understand or care about their healthcare needs. They do not clearly understand their rights, leaving them unable to advocate for themselves or their families.

It is now my life's purpose to ensure that the residents of these communities have the tools to leverage their voices to protect their health. I am determined to teach anyone and everyone who will listen how to Speak Up! Speak Out! and Speak Loud! to not only ask for but to successfully receive optimal services regardless of the color of their skin, neighborhood, or educational status.

A vivid mirage has already been painted for those I have had the opportunity to communicate with regarding the power a patient has when using their voice. The mirage changes from a vibrant, beautiful picture with a hundred unique colors where each color is telling its own story to a mundane black and white blotted photo where there is no story being told. Sadly, this represents what occurs when the patient's voice is silent. Black and brown patients, particularly women, face numerous problems and challenges in the healthcare system. It is time for the silence to end. It is time for patients to speak up and paint a vivid collage of stories that tell the truth about what they encounter when they seek medical care. Then the people in control (i.e., politicians, healthcare executives, and chief medical officers) will take note and work with the patient community to develop sustainable solutions that will decrease health inequities and disparities and increase health equity.

This book was written to show what can

happen and what does happen when a patient advocate becomes the patient. The words spoken are my personal story of how I was forced to use my voice to fight through incredibly challenging days. I chose to use COVID-19 as the backdrop for this book because it is the latest healthcare issue that has rocked this country to its core, however; it is not the only healthcare issue where the patient's voice has remained silent, and healthcare inequities and disparities have flourished. I chose to include my diary to paint the picture through the eyes of a patient of what the truth in the health care system looks like from the inside looking out. I want the readers to know that I advocate from a place of being and doing and not from a faraway place. A diary accounting of over thirty challenging days, where each day presented a different obstacle, is included in this book. The reader can see the power of the patient's voice through the recollection of an autobiographical narrative collected and presented from my diary entries.

CHAPTER 1

NO! NOT ME

The mind of man plans his way,
But God directs his steps.
—Proverbs 16:9

The article, *Demographic Health Disparities and Health System Transformation: Drivers and Solutions*[1] addresses some critical issues that highlight the gaps in care and the negative impacts on marginalized communities. The article addresses one point: "Certain populations and demographic groups suffer from illnesses or morbidities at rates disproportionately larger than the general population. This disparity exists in numerous, highly significant conditions, including obesity, diabetes, stroke, heart disease, asthma, and cancer."

People with diabetes experience various symptoms when their A1c, also known as Sugar, is not under control. There are two types of Diabetes. One classification is Diabetes Type 1. A patient's body diagnosed with Type 1 cannot make insulin on its own. Diabetic Type 1 patients rely on insulin to live. Type 1 Diabetics must have access to daily insulin injections, and failure to do so could present a life-or-death situation. The onset of this type of Diabetes usually presents in children or teens, but it can also be identified in adults.

The second classification is Type 2. The body of the Type 2 Diabetic can produce insulin, so daily injections are not needed. People with diabetes with Type 2 must take oral medications and sometimes a combination of insulin and other injectable Diabetic medication along with oral medications to control their Diabetes. Like Type 1 Diabetics, if Type 2 Diabetic does not take their medicine daily, they also face a life-threatening situation. Patients with either

Type 1 or Type 2 Diabetes must test their glucose level daily to ensure their numbers are in range. The normal range for a Diabetic varies and is based on their overall body type. I recommend that a diabetic patient have an Endocrinologist (physician specializing in caring for Diabetic patients) on their medical team. The patient and the Endocrinologist can discuss the normal range and develop a plan to ensure that the patient can make and sustain a normal glucose range. An A1C lab test (a test taken to measure a patient's glucose level over three months) is normally ordered at least every three months. This time may change depending on the patient's health status. The goal is for the test results to be no more than seven but not lower than 3.88. This is because a reading of 3.88 on a lab test indicates that the patient may have Hypoglycemia (low glucose level). Problems occur for the Diabetic patient if either Hypoglycemia (low sugar level) or Hyperglycemia (high sugar level) is present. A person with diabetes may experience various symptoms that indicate that their diabetes is out of control. Frequent urination, fatigue, and blurry vision are three of the most common. Ask me. I know all about the symptoms and how one feels when those symptoms are present. For over twenty years, at various times, I have experienced Hypoglycemic and Hyperglycemic episodic spans.

About two months before my confirmed COVID-19 diagnosis I began noticing some of the symptoms, but the sensations were different this time. I started developing feelings that I could not shake. In late 2019, a battle of extreme fatigue and an increase in the number of times I had to use the bathroom set in. My Primary Care Doctor (PCP) and Endocrinologist referred me for close to twenty lab tests to better understand and correctly diagnose what was going on within my body. In January 2020, my PCP called with the results of the tests that she had ordered. She said my cholesterol level was high, which was why I was so exhausted. She ordered medication for me and scheduled a three-month follow-up visit. I had no reason to doubt that my illness was unrelated to my medical condition.

After ending the call, I signed onto my computer and completed a Google Advanced search on the definition of high cholesterol (HDL). I wanted to know what having high cholesterol meant, and I was anxious to do whatever was necessary to overcome the extreme fatigue that I was feeling. I wrote down the steps reported by the world-renowned medical organization, Mayo Clinic2, hoping that the steps outlined in the report would help me reduce my cholesterol level. According to the article, I had to remove foods from my diet that contained trans fats and saturated (e.g., fried and processed foods, red meats, and chocolate). I had to introduce foods classified as Omega-3 rich (e.g., Salmon, Walnuts, Flax Seeds) into my diet. Exercise and adequate rest were also noted as factors in lowering cholesterol.

Armed with the information I needed to combat my diagnosis proactively, I created a game plan on the steps I would take to effectively lower my cholesterol and regain my physical and mental well-being. I began looking forward to starting the process of healing. I was happily awaiting my 25th wedding anniversary party, which my husband and I had been planning.

Over the next month, I obediently followed

the plan I had designed. I began to look and feel a little better. I still felt a sense of fatigue, but I maintained enough energy to engage in discussions with my friends and family about the day's topic, COVID-19.

Like everyone around me, I had doubts about the seriousness of the virus. The media reported instructions for people to do things I had already done, frequently washing my hands, sneezing into my elbow, and covering my mouth when I coughed. I was sure there was no way I would catch whatever this virus was going around. There were at least three reasons I mistrusted the information about the severity of the virus, but two stood out above all others. First, the political turmoil that this country was going through left me confused. I was still determining who or what to trust.

Additionally, I have always questioned stories that are reported on the news. Some journalists are senior subject matter experts on the art of spinning stories. The journalists referred to for their expertise receive all types of bonuses for the articles they write. Sometimes the stories these journalists write are false and have little truth. I can count on one hand the broadcasted stories that I have heard where there is not a slant of bias as to what is being told. Thus, I needed clarification about what was being reported. Secondly, through my studies as a graduate student in public policy, specifically the healthcare courses, I knew this was not the first pandemic this country had faced. The contextualized history and timeline I had studied had foolishly left me thinking that the United States would not be prepared for a Pandemic that would rock the nation's core.

Toward the end of February 2020, I noticed that I had lost my appetite. Whenever I would sit down to eat, I did not feel a sense of hunger. I became uninterested in enjoying the savory dishes I once ate and now would push my plate away. So, I gravitated to drinking Ensure (a supplemental nutritional shake) in the morning, noon, and night. The fatigue began to set in. I figured it was yet another diabetic obstacle and prepared myself for the onslaught of symptoms and prescriptions to combat them. One of the things that I have learned as a patient living with a chronic medical condition is that one call to a caring and professional provider regarding any healthcare challenges (i.e., fevers, weight loss, extreme fatigue) that the patient faced could be the start of numerous medical visits and testing. After spending the prior year attending one or more doctor visits per week, for about six months, due to an uncontrolled diabetic span, the last thing I wanted was to restart that cycle, so I steadfastly prayed that the fatigue would get better. I began to cringe each time I thought about any additional ailments that could be uncovered through more testing. Thus, instead of calling my primary care doctor (PCP) and informing her of my medical concerns, I quietly sat and followed a false sense of feeling better. I believed that any improvements in how I felt meant my health was improving.

Yet, day after day, my health continued to deteriorate. Daily I looked for the positive aspect of what was occurring with my health situation. I told myself that if I could not find the silver lining, I would make that dreaded call to my doctor. The Aha! moment came one day late at night. I followed a procedure that I often find comfort in whenever faced with a challenging situation. I was listening to gospel music when the lyrics started to remind me of the advantages of an employee benefit I received from my work.

Through the Family Medical Leave Act (FMLA) and an optional departmental employee perk, I could work from home at least one day a week, and if needed, I could either work an additional day at home or use the time allotted through FMLA Laws. As I thought about how blessed I was to have access to that benefit, I also thought about the conversations I had with friends and family members about the benefit and how it was in their best interest to see if it was an employee benefit, they had access to. I remember assuring them that having and using the time allotted under FMLA was a definite stress reliever.

As I started to doze off, I promised myself I would make the call to my doctor the next day. Little did I know that the days to come would prove just how beneficial my completion of the FMLA process was. I did not realize it at the time I fell asleep, but the next day when I awoke, I could sense trouble was ahead. To work from home as much as possible in the coming months, I need to combine FMLA and work work-from-home. Thank God for that blessing because I know the outcome could have been detrimental for me without it.

At the beginning of March, I received a call from my Endocrinologist inquiring about how I felt. I informed her of the increased bathroom breaks and my extreme fatigue. She immediately calmed my anxiety, advising me that it was not due to my diabetes. We had a lengthy conversation regarding the potential causes of my problems. However, COVID-19 did not make the list. Her thought was that it was a Urinary Tract Infection (UTI). She advised me to contact my PCP regarding my medical concerns and tell her that Diabetes was not the reason for my symptoms.

Furthermore, she instructed me to tell her that what she believed I was experiencing was potentially a UTI. Before ending our call, she advised me that I was at an elevated risk for

COVID-19 and suggested staying in the house away from others would be best. Neither of us pondered the notion that I had already contracted COVID-19, and my symptoms were indicative of that. Nonetheless, we mutually agreed that I would stay in the house. Once the call ended, I followed her instructions and called my PCP. I left a few messages that went unanswered before becoming irritated by the lack of response. I eventually gave up on contacting her directly. I eventually gave up trying to reach her directly. I called my Endocrinologist, hoping that she would contact my PCP on my behalf or call me back to prescribe the medication I needed to cure my presumed UTI.

I did not receive a return call from my Endocrinologist, so I sent a message through the Electronic Health Record (EHR) patient portal to both my PCP and the Endocrinologist. I was certain that I would receive a response. The Endocrinologist's office responded much faster than the PCP's. I was grateful but enraged. I wondered why the PCP had not called me back. I asked myself, does she not care about her patients and their medical concerns? Does she think that whatever I was experiencing was not an emergency?

My mind began to think of the trust and communication factors that so often mar the doctor-patient relationship, especially in the African American community. Impatiently, I began waiting for her to respond to my call. I needed an explanation as to why my calls were not being responded to. Her lack of response to my calls was raising my stress and anxiety levels, and I needed to know why my calls were not being returned.

After I called my Endocrinologist, the pharmacy called to tell me that a prescription was ready for me to pick up. I asked who had placed the prescription, and they informed me that it came from my PCP. Upon further inquiry, I discovered that the medicine ordered was to treat a UTI. I silently wondered, why would she assign medication without first diagnosing me? I was extremely sick and could not ask any questions, so I sent my husband to pick up the prescription.

An out-of-control snowball effect ensued the first full day after taking the medicine. I began developing massive headaches, my legs felt like a ton of bricks, and I could barely lift my head off the pillow. The woozy feeling I felt went on for a day before my husband called the pharmacist to ask if I should be experiencing those types of side effects. The pharmacist responded that those side effects were common with that medication and advised that I drink plenty of clear fluids and take Tylenol. My husband was also told that if my symptoms stayed the same or worsened within twenty-four hours, he should call my doctor. At no point did he indicate that I may have contracted COVID-19.

The National Coordinating Council for Medication Error Reporting and Prevention[3] (Tariq & Scherbak, 2021) defines a medication error as a "preventable event that may cause or lead to inappropriate medication use or patient harm while the medication is in the control of the healthcare professional, patient, or consumer."[2] This article points out an important fact that directly impacts marginalized communities. Medication errors are avoidable public health mistakes. Misdiagnosis and Delayed diagnosis are two of the most common medication errors, and they negatively impact communities that already have little trust in the medical community.

The lack of communication is very often at the center of medication errors. First, there is a breakdown in the communication between the medical provider who is prescribing the medication and the patient. Rarely is the patient made aware of the possible side effects of taking the medication. Additionally, they are not told what to do should they experience an anomaly. As a result, there is a breakdown in the communication between the pharmacist and the prescribing provider. In looking at what is reported to be the four most frequent medication errors: dispensing an incorrect medication, dosage strength, or dosage form; miscalculating a dose; and failing to identify drug interactions or contraindications4 (AMCP, 2019). it is evident that the pharmacist is often unfairly blamed for the lack of patient care. Sadly, a result of this lack of communication between the professional entities presents a matter of life or death for the patient. Statistically speaking, in the United States, over eight thousand people die per year from medication errors, and thousands of patients have allergic reactions to medications but do not report the adverse reaction or other medication complications they experience. Billions are spent on providing care for patients that have suffered complications due to medication errors. Along with the financial cost involved, there is also the socioeconomic pain that patients experience, which is related to medication errors5 (Tariq & Scherbak, 2021).

At the beginning of the month, I had a perfect plan in hand and began working on positive health changes. I felt rejuvenated in my spirit, and hope settled in; I was on my way to a healthier me. So, it came as a shocking surprise that, within two weeks, I was diagnosed with COVID-19.

The fury, disappointment, and confusion that ran through my veins when I learned of the diagnosis created a melting pot of emotional trauma. I did not know whether to be upset with my PCP, the pharmacist, or my Endocrinologist.

They each knew about my health concerns, but I felt as though each one of them had carelessly passed my health concerns off as an inconvenience they needed to alleviate and move on from.

Fight! I tell people who are facing uphill challenges dealing with the American healthcare system. This is a global word of encouragement. Marginalized communities exist in all countries. Far too many people are being silenced when it comes to requesting that medical providers treat them just like they were a member of their own families. This should not happen, but sadly it does.

Patient-Centered Care is a term often spoken whenever an attempt to paint a positive picture of the patient experience is being discussed. The actions being carried out tell a different story. One reason for this is that no one has explained this concept of care to the patient population; thus, sadly, many patients have no idea of the power their voice holds in terms of asking, requesting, and getting excellent health care.

Never give up! Doing so will not fix the healthcare system. The exact opposite will occur. Gaps in access to high medical care and subpar medical treatment will continue to thrive in marginalized communities if we give up. Following this mantra is what gave me the physical and mental strength to fight through a month filled with fear, intimidation, and determination.

I opine that there are at least three reasons why a patient, especially a hospitalized patient, should keep a medical diary/journal. Once I realized that my mental energy was not at full capacity, I began a journal on how this virus was depleting me wholistically. While authoring this book, I reflected on the notes I had made, and while I may not have realized it at the time, the three reasons I give for the importance of a patient keeping a journal/diary must be implanted in my head. The rational thought behind each of these reasons surfaced continuously through the many notes I had taken. Those three ideas are inclusive of the following: First, maintaining a diary allows the patient to recall the events that led up to them seeking medical care. Second, recording in a medical journal/ diary allows the patient to process their own thoughts and feelings about the illness they are experiencing and how the relationship they are having with the clinical team that has been charged to return their condition a patient to optimal health status. Third, it allows for the patient to release any pent-up feelings in words rather than staging a verbal altercation. Stress factors such as anxiety and tension often lead to a sense of frustration. Writing those thoughts down in a medical diary/ journal allows the patient to avoid a verbal altercation which could result in even more frustration.

CHAPTER 2

WHAT AN UNFORGETTABLE MONTH!

*Be on your guard; stand firm in
the faith; be courageous; be
strong.*
—1 Corinthians 16:13

DIARY ENTRY: DAY 1

Friday, March 27, 2020, is a day that will be forever etched in my mind. As always, I was up at 6:30 am preparing for the day ahead. I had just spent the past few days at home from work resting as I was beginning to feel worse than I had felt over the prior two weeks. I had lost my appetite to the point where day after day, I was getting my nutrition from drinking a Nutritional Supplement for breakfast, lunch, and dinner. I was unable to fight off the constant feeling of fatigue. While the use of acetaminophen was helpful in reducing my fever, there was still a battle within my body and mind that told me that I needed to seek care through the Emergency Room. It had to have been about 11:00 am when I realized I was in no condition to continue working. As the clock continued to tick, I noticed that I was putting little effort into completing any work. I also noticed that my body was longing to shut down completely. Thus, I wrapped up my work for the day, signed out of my computer, and proceeded towards my bedroom, where I planned to nap. The next thing I knew, my husband was waking me up. He heard me struggling to breathe and wanted to know if I was ok. I struggled to respond, and it must have been within that moment that he feared that if I continued to lay there, I would have slipped further into oblivion. Not wanting to take any more chances, he encouraged me to wake up and get dressed so that he could take me to the Emergency Room. Five hours later, I managed to muster enough strength to put my clothes on so that I could head to the hospital.

Upon my arrival, I was triaged and diagnosed with pneumonia. In addition, I was evaluated for COVID-19 and advised that the results would not be ready for 24 hours, but since I had pneumonia, I would need to be admitted to the hospital. A deeper evaluation of my symptoms showed that in addition to having pneumonia, my oxygen level was low. As a result, I was placed on IV and oxygen tubing. The clinical team told me and my husband that I would be kept in the ER until a bed was ready for me. At about 11:00 pm, the bed was ready, and then the fear began to set in. That unsettling feeling of fear became real when we were told that, due to the risk of him becoming infected, he would not be able to accompany me or visit while I was a patient. I am not sure what time it was, but I recall overhearing a conversation at the nurse's station a few hours later, which was right outside my room, where the word positive was used, and then a few minutes later, a sign that said positive went up on my door. A nurse then came into my room and asked if I had overheard the conversation regarding my confirmed diagnosis. I responded yes, but I was taken aback because I had been told just hours ago that my results would not be back for another 24 hours. I closed my eyes and began to sleep because I was too tired and exhausted to ask questions.

DIARY ENTRY: DAY 2

Today is Saturday, March 28, 2020, and it is my first full day of hospitalization. I have not yet grasped the reality of my situation, but I am becoming keenly aware that I am going to be victorious in pulling through. To be heard as a patient, I will need all of God's grace and as much patience as I can muster. In my role as a patient advocate, I constantly encourage patients to use their voice. It is becoming apparent that I will need to use my own words of advice to ensure that I receive optimal health care.

Right now, I am physically and emotionally drained. I admit I am weak but notice the obstacles and challenges that keep reoccurring. Silently I tell myself to take notes on all that is happening. Thank God I have a good understanding of the relationship between better health outcomes and patient empowerment. Being aware of that dynamic has armed me with the determination to fight through all the nuisances that I have experienced today.

My day started when the assigned nurse woke me up so that I could take my medication. There were two pills that she needed me to take. I was not told what the medicine was; I was only told why I was taking it. The nurse advised me that it was to treat the COVID-19 infection. I was not given a choice of medication or told the name of the drug. I also did not have anyone to advocate for the type of medication I was given as I was self-isolated. Since I was weak from fighting the fever and my oxygen level was low, I felt like I had no choice but to take the medication I was given. I had been following the news before my admission into the hospital. I put two and two together to realize that the medication I was being treated with was the same medication that was consistently being debated on TV.

The debates regarding the efficacy of the medication would have been fine, but I was bothered by the arguments that focused on the financial profits that were being realized by the manufacturers and the company stockholders.

After I had finished taking my medication, the nurse told me about the COVID-19 floor procedures. She apologetically advised me that if I needed help from a nurse or doctor, I would need to use the telephone handset she provided me. I was told that the reason for this was that due to a lack of knowledge regarding the transmission of COVID-19 that face-to-face patient/clinician time would be minimized. Simply put, everyone was fearful of encountering the unknown. It was determined that reducing interaction was the best way to keep the virus at bay. Unless an emergency arose, the only time a nurse would be coming into my room was at the beginning and end of a shift.

Additionally, there were no nurses who were COVID-19 trained. As a result, I may not have the same nurse each day. It occurred to me that I would need to adopt an attitude of patience when requesting and receiving help for anything I would need. Once I had completed taking my medication, the nurse brought me my breakfast tray. I still did not have an appetite, so I did not want anything heavy. I just wanted my En-sure. I picked through the meal tray that I was brought and just ate a handful of the potatoes. Since I do not eat pork, I could not eat the Ham that was on the tray. The bread was hard and cold. Also, a no-go was the whole milk and the coffee. I was hoping to see a menu on the tray to order my lunch meal but soon found out that COVID-19 patients could not choose options from a menu but were served whatever was be-ing cooked for the day unless otherwise noted in their chart. I let my assigned nurse know that I did not eat pork and that I did not want food that required effort in swallowing as I had no appetite in the hopes that she would relay this to the dietary department.

Soon after the nurse left, I visited an attend-ing physician face-to-face. To say this physician was unprofessional is an understatement. I had never seen this doctor before, and from the way she abruptly tossed me on my side to keep from looking me in my face, I could tell she had no bedside manners. Once she exited my room, I immediately called the nursing station and filed a complaint. I did not want that doctor back in my room. I spoke with the nurse who answered the phone and told her what had just occurred with the doctor. I voiced my concern about being treated as anything less than human and requested another doctor be assigned to oversee my care. I was not going to be denied proper patient care. I was pleasantly surprised and grateful to have my voice heard and my request granted. Within the hour, I received a call from my newly assigned physician. In reflecting back on this incident, I shudder to think what would have happened had I not opened my mouth and placed the complaint.

Hours later, it was lunchtime. The lunch tray was no better than the breakfast. I paged my nurse to advise her that I would not eat what I had been brought. I asked her what number to call for the dietary department. She provided the number, and I called to advise them of my dietary restrictions. I was asked what I wanted for lunch, and since the potatoes were all I ate that morning for breakfast, I told them potatoes. Realizing that I would not get stronger if I did not eat, I asked the dietician to place me on a soft diet. I was advised that a doctor would need to send an order for me to be switched to a liquid or soft diet. I thanked her for taking the time to call me back and ended the call. Immediately after ending the call, I paged the doctor and explained my dilemma with the meals that I had been brought that day. I advised him that the food was not appeasing and that I could eat anything other than the potatoes. I told him that I would prefer not to eat a solid meal because I did not have an appetite. I pleaded with him to put me on a soft diet so I could receive nourishment. I was really hoping that he would put me back on my Ensure, but that is not what happened. All was not lost because he did agree to the soft diet, just without the Ensure. Minutes after ending the call with the doctor, the dietician called me back. She advised me that she had received the order for me to proceed with a soft diet but thought it best to set up a menu plan for when I was able to resume eating from a regular diet. Thus, we planned a meal menu, which I was initially unhappy with. My unhappiness with the planned menu was because instead of the nutritional supplement Ensure that I had been drinking on the regular for the past month, she was more encouraging of the less sugary Glucerna and fruits and vegetables.

Shortly after ending the call with the dietician, I called the nurse's desk and placed a prayer request. Later in the day, a minister called, and after we briefly spoke and joined in a virtual holding of hands, we then proceeded in prayer. I needed to focus my mind on spiritual healing. I needed to hear the whisper of those words that God loved me and was there with me holding my hand and guiding me through this storm. I needed to listen to those words because I was sure that his grace would become my guiding light.

Additionally, I would need to recall those words and use them as words of encouragement to keep going when I felt tempted to let the virus take over. I needed to ask God to heal me and protect my family and loved ones from this horrific virus. I needed to be reminded of those words written in Psalm 30 verse 5 that "weeping may endure for a night, but joy cometh in the morning." Shortly after the prayer ended, I felt a complete stillness. A wave of relief washed over me. I no longer worried about not physically seeing my husband or being a patient who was being challenged with the unknown. I was confident that God was in control.

The remainder of the day was uneventful until dinner time. The first noticeable change was that my dinner tray had nothing but soft foods. My tray consisted of Chocolate and Vanilla pudding, Fruit Salad, Mashed Potatoes, Apple Juice, Fruit Punch, and a roll. I quizzically looked at the tray as I was confused. Everything that was on the tray was full of sugar. Indeed, I thought they had made a mistake. I questioned myself on how they could bring a person with diabetes a tray full of sugar.

Shortly after I had eaten, I took my evening medications. Sleep followed shortly thereafter. It must have been a deep slumber as I drifted into a dream. According to scientific data, the type of dream I had is frequently reported by those who tested positive for COVID-19. My dream was symbolic in that both of my oldest sisters, who are now deceased, appeared. One was on my left side, and one was on my right side. The sister on my left told me that my life's work was not done and that she was not ready for me to join her. She told me to wake up. She kissed me on my cheek, and her clear image faded. My sister, who was on the right, then appeared. She asked me a question she had asked me once before when I was sick. She asked me who gave me permission to give up and not fight for my life when it was challenged. She reminded me that God was in control. She told me to stop worrying and rest up as I had a fight in front of me, and I would need all my strength to come out victorious. She started humming the tune "Hush Little Baby," and then her image faded away. A spiritual whisper followed. The dialogue with the whisperer did not last long, but it was a direct dialogue. I was told that my work here on earth was not done. When I asked, "what work?" The answer was that I had been given a gift from God, and I was expected to use it. When I asked what the gift was, I was told that I knew what that gift was, and then the dialogue ended. I then lay awoke for a few moments before drifting into a quiet, peaceful sleep. It was as if I was wrapped in a warm cocoon.

DAIRY ENTRY: DAY 3

Sunday, March 29, 2020, is day three of my hospitalization. I began thinking long and hard about my symbolic dream last night after waking up this morning. My thoughts soon became fixated on the phrase, "Your Next is Now." I questioned myself as to why my thoughts were focused on that phrase. The words whispered from God that I knew what my gift was kept replaying in my head. I knew that the gift I was being encouraged to use had something to do with health care, but I am unsure how to unwrap the gift that God gave me and use it most beneficially. There were options that I had at the ready.

One option would be to help others recover funds that people had paid to medical providers that should not have been paid. Another option would be to use my gift of researching medical documentation to help someone obtain the medical treatment they need to prolong their life. There was also my gift for helping others find healthcare resources when they had reached the brink of giving up and giving in to suffering needlessly in pain. The people I had helped in the past who fell into this category were either elderly or those society has labeled as down-trodden.

As I contemplated the various routes I could take in using my God-given gift to be a blessing to others, I took a deep breath and slowly ex-haled. I knew that there would be rough days ahead for dealing with this virus, but I also knew there would be good days. I knew that be-fore I could help others, I would have to fully recover from this devastating illness. Thus, I si-lently prayed that God's grace would pull me through the storm that I was in the middle of so that I could be a blessing to others.

Throughout the day, I have been experienc-ing a profound sense of anxiety, anticipation, and fear. The fear was because I was exhaust-ed, but I was too afraid to get the deep sleep I needed. I kept hearing horror stories on the news about the increase in people dying from this awful virus. I kept seeing patients on ventilators being wheeled past my room. I was afraid that if I fell into a deep sleep, I would not wake up, or if I did wake up, I would be placed on a ventilator. So, I have willed myself just to take brief naps throughout the day. Unfortunately, in doing that, I am driving my anxiety to an unhealthy level. The glass half full instead of empty philosophy that I live by is helping to calm my anxiousness. This may be the reason I am finding myself anxious with anticipation. The days prior to being hospitalized with COVID-19 were scary. I made a promise to myself that if I were blessed to survive this virus, things in my life would change, and I would make sure that they changed for the better.

DIARY ENTRY: DAY 4

I open my eyes with anticipation for a new day. It is now March 30, 2020. The last three days have been busy days. The constant hustling that I am used to has come to a screeching halt. I have no choice but to sit still with my thoughts and reflect on my life. Today, I woke up with a sense of anxiety and anticipation, but I was more serene and at peace. I had decided to accept this turmoil I was in and ride it out for as long as necessary. That sense of serenity lasted about an hour. Before I knew it, the floodgates of misery and disaster had swung wide open, and from that point on, I have been miserably moving through the day. I do not think I will ever forget this day. It started with me having an extreme case of indigestion. In addition, I am still having a tough time going to the bathroom. I have not been able to eliminate any kind of waste from my body. I miss my husband, and this hospital bed is nothing like my nice bed at home.

I was becoming frustrated. The doctor had started talking about discharging me. He was pleased with the lab numbers he saw, and I no longer had a fever. He was also quite pleased to see that my oxygen intake was under control. He relayed to me the optimistic feeling he was having about sending me home before the week ended. He encouraged me to start sitting up and trying to walk around the room to stabilize myself. I mentioned to him that I was concerned about not using the bathroom, and he responded that the time would come when this problem would no longer be present. Determined to make it happen sooner than later, I must have drunk about 3 gallons of water today. I drank a lot of water, yet for some reason, it took a while to use the bathroom. Even walking around the room has not been helpful. I walked around this room twice, and nothing happened. I sat up in the chair for what have been an hour, not writing anything but looking out into the world, yearning desperately to be a part of the outside world. This tired me out to the point that I needed rest. Thus, I rose from the chair, went to bed, and took a nap.

Hours later, my assigned nurse gave me my afternoon medication and brought me my lunch tray. She inquired as to how I was doing. I confessed to her that I was exhausted; the walking and sitting were too much for me. She advised me to take it easy and not be so hard on myself. She does not know that I always push myself past exertion when there is a goal I am trying to reach. She has no idea that I will not take it easy until I can eliminate the bodily waste that has been inside me for far too long. Only then would I know that my destination of being discharged home was a reality and not just something I wanted. Once the nurse left, I began to drink more water. I drank water until I was ready to burst. I was determined that I was going to use the bathroom before the day ended. Later in the day, the nurse called to see how I was doing and let me know that she was leaving for the day. She bid me wishes for a speedy and healthy recovery; I thanked her, and we ended the call.

After the call ended, I thanked God for placing me in the care of someone who cared about her patients. I spent the rest of the day watching television, making phone calls to relatives and friends, writing in my diary, hoping to go to the bathroom, and attempting to get some uninterrupted sleep.

DIARY ENTRY: DAY 5

The date reads March 31, 2020, on the calendar. I am unsure how it happened, but I have lost complete track of the days. That is when I realize that I am extremely exhausted. I am silently praying that today is not a repeat of yesterday. I am not sure how much longer I can stay in this hospital. Four days of repetitive challenges and issues are enough for me. It is day five, and I am at my wit's end. I am not sure how much more I can take. Endless days and nights have been thrust upon me, and I am ready to go home. For close to a week, I have been separated from the comforts of home. I have been away from my husband for five days and am lonely. The laughter and conversation of face-to-face interaction with him are missing, and I am beginning to become frustrated with the upheaval that this virus has forced me into. I find myself questioning why I am still here. I am confused as to why I must have a bowel movement before they consider discharging me.

Yesterday, the doctor started talking about discharging me. He was pleased with the lab numbers he saw, and I no longer had a fever. He was also quite pleased to see that my oxygen intake was under control. He relayed to me the optimistic feeling he was having about sending me home before the week ended. He encouraged me to start sitting up and trying to walk around the room to stabilize myself. I mentioned to him that I was concerned about not using the bathroom, and he responded that the time would come when this problem would no longer be present. Determined to make it happen sooner than later, I began drinking as what seemed like an unsurmountable amount of water. Once again, all the water I drank did nothing to propel me to use the bathroom. Like yesterday, I walked around the room, which was absolutely no help. After walking around the room twice, I then decided to sit up in the chair in my room. I sat up, looking outside. I am not sure if it was annoyance or tiredness, but staring out the window left me completely exhausted. As a result, I got up from the chair and went to bed to take a nap. My designated nurse brought my lunch plate and my afternoon pill a few hours later. She asked how I was feeling. I admitted to her that I was feeling stressed. She advised me to take it easy and not be so hard on myself. She did not know why I was pushing myself so hard. She had no idea that I was eager to have bodily waste eliminated. Only then would I know that my destination of being discharged home was a reality and not just something I wanted. Once the nurse left, I began to drink more water. I drank water until I was ready to burst. I was determined that I was going to use the bathroom before the day ended. Within the hour, the nurse called to see how I was doing and let me know that she was leaving for the day. She bid me wishes for a speedy and healthy recovery. I thanked her, and we ended the call. After the call ended, I thanked God for placing me in the care of someone who cared about her patients.

At about 6:30 pm, my evening nurse came in to check on me. I was sitting in the chair when he entered my room. He found me a bit agitated as it was well past my dinner time. I immediately noticed his nervousness and told him I was hungry and had not eaten dinner. I also told him that my bed had not been made up all day and that I had not yet washed up. He apologized for being late and proceeded to check my vitals and give me my evening meds. Once that was done, I told him that I was tired, but I wanted to sit up, eat dinner, wash up, and then lay down. After he had finished getting his clinical information, he quickly brought me my dinner tray and stated that he would be back shortly to make up my bed and help me wash up for the evening. He then left the room. After waiting close to an hour, I decided that I had had enough of sitting up and waiting for him to return. I pushed my tray from before me, slowly raised from the chair, and headed to the bed. I laid in bed for a while before I finally had to use the bathroom. I pushed the intercom and advised the nurse who answered the telephone that I needed help going to the bathroom. He responded that my nurse would be right there to help. I waited a while, and then when the nurse did not come, I again pushed the intercom and requested assistance from the nurse.

Still, no nurse came. Unable to stop the waste from coming, I let it go, remembering that I had a catheter designed to help catch it. Unbeknownst to me, the catheter had broken and was useless. As the water began to flow increasingly out of my body, I managed to press the intercom one final time. The nurse that had told me over an hour ago that the nurse was on his way answered the call and angrily told him what had occurred and that I was laying in my own waste. I told him it had been close to an hour since I placed the first call asking for help and that no nurse had come to my room. I was now frustrated and annoyed. Never in my life had something this humiliating happened to me. I prayed to God that someone would soon show up and help me out of the puddle of waste that I was lying in. At that moment, I made a promise to myself that this would not happen again. Right after making that call, the nurse came into the room. He apologized, but it did not help. That situation was avoidable. I told the nurse that no one should be subjected to inhumane conditions. I prayed that neither myself nor anyone else would ever find themselves in a situation like this. The nurse proceeded to help me get out of the now-soaked bed, wash up, and change the bedding. Needless to say, This day ended with my level of frustration notched up a level or two, but through the hurt and humiliation, I had a testimony to give. I was still alive.

It could have been much worse.

After calming myself down, I prayed that God gives me the strength to move past this incident and continue to gain the strength needed to heal. I also prayed that God would provide me with a spirit of forgiveness toward those who had the opportunity to stop this incident from occurring and either would not or could not get to me in time to be of help.

DIARY ENTRY: DAY 6

Today is April 1, 2020. I woke up this morning with three things on my mind. One is to call the hospital administration department. They will get an earful of my complaining. What happened to me should not happen to another patient. Secondly, I need to talk with the doctor. I have been here for six days. Repeatedly, I keep hearing that they are waiting for me to have a bowel movement. I have had one now, so I am eager to hear about the delay. I understand that they are not to blame for my current situation, but I am sick of being here and want to go home.

Third, checking on my people is imperative. Selfishly, I have not been thinking about anything but myself. I have not paid much attention to the stories that have been broadcasted throughout the day, but I have heard enough to know that the sign of disparity through lack of access to care is negatively impacting the lives of those who live in the Black and brown communities. People are being turned away from receiving care, or they are not receiving the right type of care, and I cannot access my bullhorn to send them in the right direction for them to get the care they need.

Most of my day was uneventful. I was glad to have a day where I could rest and take stock of what lay ahead of me once discharged from the hospital. My doctor called and checked to see how I was doing. He was enthusiastic about the lab results he was receiving. He asked if I was ready to go home. I excitedly told him I was, although I knew I had not yet reached the measurable points publicized by the Centers for Disease Control for the infectious stage. Those things included being fever-free for a minimum of three days without using a pain reliever, being cough-free without taking cough medicine, and being at ease in breathing with minimum oxygen assistance. Thus, I knew that the question the doctor asked was being done so out of courtesy. My symptoms were beginning to abate, so if things remained, the earliest I would be discharged was tomorrow. Just talking about going home was exciting for me. The sooner I was released, the earlier I could start working on my assignment from God.

The joy and peaceful morning that I was able to enjoy quickly disappeared that afternoon and evening. It all began with a pinching sensation I started to feel in my arm where the IV had been placed. The pain level I was experiencing told me that something was wrong. After giving it, some thought, I remembered that last night, when the prior nurse went to place the IV in my arm, she struggled with finding a proper IV placement spot. The pain was bothering me so bad that I attempted to pull the IV out. It looked as if the arm with the IV was beginning to swell. Luckily for me, the evening nurse had just entered my room. I immediately told her about the pain I was feeling. She looked at the site and how the IV was placed and said that it had been put in wrong. She removed the IV and placed it in the other arm. I breathed a huge sigh of relief.

After the nurse left my room, my thoughts immediately turned to the principle of Patient Safety, which is highly encouraged in the healthcare profession. It is the science of keeping the patient safe from harm, and this incident left me wondering if the Patient Safety protocols were being reviewed with the clinical team. I realize that these are trying times, but the healthcare provider should own up to any errors they make or not serve in the capacity of being a care provider. Failure to do so places the patient in an at-risk position.

DIARY ENTRY: DAY 7

Today is April 2, 2020. I have been catapulted into my seventh day of hospitalization. I awoke with nervous anticipation. Eagerly, I anticipate being told that this is my day of discharge. The benchmarks of having no fever, being cough free, and having an oxygen level of ninety percent for the past three days have been met. The nervousness of my current situation is because I am still in the infectious stage. According to the Centers for Disease Control (CDC) website, the infectious period is fourteen days. Clinically, I understand that all illnesses have an incubation period, but I find the information regarding this virus a bit confusing. I have questioned my doctor and the assigned nurses on when the fourteen-day start period begins, and each of them has directed me to the Centers for Disease Control (cdc.gov) website. Researching information on that website for various health conditions usually returns a plethora of information. Looking up the data on COVID-19 proved just the opposite for me. There was a ton of information, only this time, I found the information not to be conclusive. It is disheartening to me that when I ask the doctor or the nursing team what the protocol is for the start and end day of the infectious period, the only answer I get is to check for the information posted on cdc.gov. All I am asking for is when the 14-day period starts. I am not sure why they cannot just say they do not know. I would prefer that versus sending me to a website that has the same information they have. I am not going to learn the truth. Thus, I have learned to count the days that are conclusive such as the periods for fever, oxygen, and coughing. As a result, I know for sure that it is time for discharge day.

Counting down on the minutes and seconds when I would receive the call, acknowledging what I already knew meant the start of a waiting game. This allowed me free time to give a deep reflection on whether I was fully prepared to go home. Anxious and apprehensive were just two of the feelings that were flooding my mind this morning. I was still considered to be infectious. This meant that the possibility of infecting my husband could occur. Was I being selfish in wanting to go home? Was it better for me to remain in the hospital, quarantined away from the outside world? As I thought about these two questions, I noticed that the word fear started to enter my consciousness.

I was fearful in that I did not know what was ahead for me. Guilt! Was my immediate response to the thought of bringing the evil germ of the COVID-19 virus into my home and passing it on to my husband. I wondered if he contracts the virus will I have the same strength he had in caring for me and be just as vital to him? I am starting to rethink my haste in wanting to go home. I can hide my fear of that occurring away from the outside world in the hospital, but once discharged, I will not be able to hide that fear. The sense of anxiety that I was feeling was because I wanted to get back to the real world. I yearned to sleep in my bed and eat my food. I desired to be surrounded by the things that meant the most to me, such as listening to gospel music and moving to my own beat. I wanted to see happy people and feel the positive energy of those with whom I was close. I yearned to sleep in my bed and eat my food. Watching as people sicker than me were being wheeled past my room, both on and off ventilators, was beginning to depress me.

Spirituality seemed to be the peace that was holding all the other thought processes in check. The praise I felt came from knowing that it was God's grace that had blessed me through this storm that was ending. Wholistically I was still weak, but I was in better shape than when they admitted me. I told myself that it could only get better from here. The erasure of those negative words that were crowding my brain would disappear with faith and prayer.

As I was waiting to be discharged, I began paying close attention to a harried pace on the floor that my room was on. There appeared to be more patients being admitted to the hospital today, some in worse condition than I was and some in the same state as me. In the nurses' expressions, I could see the urgency on their faces. I even had conversations with my assigned nurses about the long hours they were working to keep patients alive and how an uptick in the number of people being admitted to the hospital with a positive diagnosis was occurring. I knew that all the clinicians, not just the nurses, were fatigued and was appreciative that they still found the time to check on me, but I knew that their time could be better utilized caring for the newly admitted patients. I had two routes that I could choose from regarding going home. The first choice was to tell my doctor that I felt a few extra days spent in the hospital would be more beneficial to me, and the second choice was to proceed with being discharged from the hospital. It was during that time that I knew my purpose for being in the hospital had passed. I also removed all doubt and uncertainty about being discharged home at that time. Yes! I was ready to go home.

DIARY ENTRY: DAY 8

Today is April 3, 2020. Disappointed is how I woke up this morning. I am saddened by the fact that I am still in this hospital. This is day eight. The feelings I had yesterday dissipated as I went to sleep, realizing that the hope I had held out for being discharged amounted to wasted time and energy. I am resigned to stop the dreaming that I have been going through for the past few days. Patience is going to be added to my action vocabulary from this point forward.

Consciously I would lower my anxiety level. Subduing my anxiety level would help with eliminating the fear. Cool, calm, and collected is my new mode of Operandi. At least, that was what I was telling myself. Shortly after accepting the defeat of the situation, my doctor called and inquired about how I was feeling. Not wanting to set me up for another letdown, I responded, "ok." Next, he asked if I was ready to go home. Resoundingly, I said yes! He shared with me that based on the excellent lab results he was receiving; he saw no reason I should remain in the hospital and that he would proceed with signing the discharge papers. He then wished me well and ended the call. Within an hour of ending the call, I received my first call from the discharge nurse. She advised me that she was working to fulfill the two orders that the doctor had requested. One of the orders was for me to be sent home with oxygen. The second order was to attempt to find an at-home nurse. She told me finding the oxygen vendor would be easy but finding a nursing agency that would be able to fill the second order would be hard. The justification she gave for the difficulty in securing a private duty nurse was due to the risk that a nurse would be coming into my home when I was still contagious. She told me that once she had confirmed the delivery of the oxygen, the doctor would give me the approval to be discharged, and the search for a nursing agency would be continued once I was at home.

About an hour later, I received a second call from the discharge nurse advising me that everything was set for me to go home. We talked briefly about the importance of finishing the medication cycle that was started while I was in the hospital. I only had one other pill to take, and the chances of relapse should I not finish the medication precisely as prescribed were high. She also advised me to get rest and drink plenty of clear fluids once I was released from the hospital. I told her not to worry and that I would follow the discharge orders she gave me. The last thing I wanted to do was to be readmitted to the hospital. I received the final discharge call about an hour after the last call. Shortly thereafter, I was wheeled through what I call the COVID-19 exit. This exit was only used by COVID-19 patients leaving the hospital. The intention was to minimize the interaction between Covid patients and others. I had mixed feelings as I exited the wheelchair and stepped into my husband's waiting car. I was excited to be going home, but I silently prayed for nothing but the best for the wonderful nurses who treated me with love and compassion during my stay.

On our way home, my husband and I made a stop at the pharmacy to pick up my medication. Despite being advised by the discharge nurse that the script for the medication had been sent to the pharmacy during the afternoon, we soon found out that was not the case. The technician stated that we could come back in about an hour and the medication would be ready. My husband advised the technician that I had just been released from the hospital and that it would be impossible for either me or him to return in an hour to pick up the medicine. My husband explained to the technician the importance of the medication. He asked us to wait while he spoke with the pharmacist. The pharmacist arrived a few minutes later and told us that if we could wait outside in our car for about twenty minutes, he would prepare the medication. We had no choice but to wait as I was unwilling to chance a return visit to the hospital. So, within the first hour after my discharge, I had already broken my guarantee to the discharge nurse that I would rest. This should have been my first clue that my transition home from the hospital would not be restful.

After picking up my medication, we then proceeded home. About twenty minutes after arriving home, we received a call from the Durable Medical Equipment supplier regarding my oxygen delivery. It did not take long for the delivery to arrive. Within an hour, the oxygen was delivered and left on our front porch. The technician did not enter the home but called and advised that it was set outside and that if we had any questions on the correct usage, we could call customer service, and they would walk us through the proper setup. So, the second hour of my transition home was spent with my husband on the phone with customer service, learning how to correctly set up the oxygen so that I would be able to rest and recover at home comfortably. My husband had safely secured the oxygen tubing by the end of the call. Tired and weak, I fell fast asleep once the oxygen was connected. This process provided me with another clue that my transition home was not going to be restful. This was clue number two that rest was not going to come easy for me. However, it was utterly lost on me, just like the first clue.

Everyone needs an advocate is a mantra that all advocates know. Additionally, it is a fact. Unfortunately, the healthcare system and many patients have never heard of this mantra. It would be wise for the healthcare system to proactively encourage this mantra to patients, their families, and their loved ones before they are discharged and not retroactively once they are home. The responsibility that a hospital has ends once the patient is discharged.

See no evil! Hear no evil! Know no evil! is what the patient/provider relationship resembles once a patient is discharged from the hospital. It is rare to find a hospital system concerned enough about a patient's post-discharge care status to call that patient after discharge. As a result, many patients are left to fend for themselves once they are no longer admitted. Many of these patients are readmitted to the hospital because they lack the resources needed to follow the instructions given to them during the discharge process. Additionally, patients, especially those from marginalized communities, have no way of avoiding the social determinants of healthcare, such as transportation to and from providers for follow-up visits, access to paying for and/or picking up prescribed medications, and home safety issues after they are discharged. This does not need to happen. Ensuring a patient has someone they can call and ask for help accessing post-discharge resources can help a patient fully heal without worrying about readmission. One way to do this is for healthcare systems to do a better job of working with outside Independent Professional Advocate businesses that can offer the services needed to ensure that patients receive great follow-up care.

CHAPTER 3

THE COMFORTS OF HOME

*My people will abide in a peaceful
habitation, in secure dwellings,
and in quiet resting places.
-Isaiah 32:18*

DIARY ENTRY:DAY 9

Today is April 4th, 2020. Waking up in my own bed feels so good. I certainly do not miss waking up in the middle of the night to have blood drawn. Sleeping alone was no fun, but my husband and I cannot sleep in the same bed due to my infection status. Smelling the freshly cooked food left me giddy with excitement. No more sugar-filled foods. My husband pacing in the kitchen and then placing a breakfast tray at the bedroom door caused me to stop and thank God for the wonderful support my husband pro-vided for me. Momentarily, I would attempt to get up and make it to the bedroom door, but I seriously doubted that would happen. Tossing and turning in my bed as I was unable to sleep left me extremely exhausted. There were two reasons that I could think of that kept me from a good night's sleep. One reason was that my oxygen level seemed to have dropped. Secondly, I still could not believe that the dark days that proceeded me were behind me. Honestly, there were days when I did not believe that I would make it through to the next day.

Hopefully, what is on that plate can be easily reheated. I can use a fulfilling meal. My mind and my body are not coordinated. I need them to align so that I can get up and get to that plate of food. Until then, I will just have to lie right here. The only way I can even feel myself trying to raise up is to use the bathroom, and right now, I have no need to do that.

I find it funny that as much as I want to eat, my body is forcing me to sleep. Before long, that is exactly what happens as it is now noon, and I can hear my husband knocking on the bedroom door asking me if I am ok. He tells me he became worried when I had not eaten break-fast. Speaking to the door, I respond that I am ok, only tired as I had not slept well on the prior evening. I muster enough strength to rise and head toward the door. Not surprisingly, he had reheated the food and left me a bottle of water so that I could take my medicine along with the newspaper to read. I could certainly get used to this. After taking a sponge bath and eating, I began to watch television. Then my phone be-gan to ring. It was my external support network calling to check on me. Talking is one of my fa-vorite pastimes hobbies so I am going to try and talk with everyone that calls.

Support networks are important. Constant encouragement has a positive impact on a per-son as they are going through the healing pro-cess. They can also drain the energy from those about whom they are worried. Passing along well-meaning thoughts is the goal, but calling and trying to talk to someone whose body is weakened puts an additional strain on healing. A lesson I thought that I had learned while in the hospital was to limit the amount of time I spent talking because it tired me out, but now that I am home, I am feeling like I can keep enjoying my favorite hobby, which is talking incessantly. I am starting to feel lightheaded. I am not sure who the last person was that I was conversing with on the phone. I am starting to feel that talking is overexerting my body before I knew it, I was fast asleep. I hear my phone beeping when I awake. Note to self: you are not ready to hold multiple or lengthy conversations. I spent the rest of the day resting and texting versus vocal calling.

DIARY ENTRY:DAY 10

Sunday, April 5, 2020. On Tap, another restful day! Text chatting, resting, listening to gospel music, and finding a virtual church service are on my agenda for the day. I am looking forward to enjoying another peaceful day. I plan to take full advantage of this final day of rest. No one does business over the weekend, so my phone will remain quiet. I will have time today to catch up on my journal entries. Since I am not sure who will be calling on Monday or what type of temperament the caller will have, I need to prepare myself for the day ahead. Thus, I will be spending the day in full chill mode.

Last night was another rough evening. Restless sleep was once again present. Catnaps throughout the evening were helpful in making it through the evening. I could not figure out why my oxygen level was dropping during the evening, but in the morning, I was able to comfortably breathe, although; occasionally, I noticed a shortness of breath.

After eating and sponge bathing, I proceeded to enjoy the day. Interruption free, yes, for me. Something tells me that I will need all the strength I can to persevere through the upcoming days.

DIARY ENTRY:DAY 11

It is Monday, April 6, 2020, and I am shocked back to reality. Just as I expected, a deluge of calls start coming in. Buckle up for the ride is what I thought to myself. There will be no smooth ride to recovery. That ride ended the moment I was discharged. The rollercoaster ride that all patients ride on has just begun.

The chain of events that occurred on the first work weekday at home started a pattern that may have led me to seek mental health services if not for my over 30 years of healthcare experience. The scenario made me realize that I would need all my strength and voice to fight for the rest that I needed if I were truly going to heal from COVID-19. I was truly thankful to God that I endured the educational and personal triumphs that taught me the challenges I would soon face head-on.

The day started with me receiving one of the many calls I would receive from one of the two nurses with whom I had the pleasure of building a relationship as I maneuvered my way through COVID-19. My health insurance company's nurse was the first to call. After she verified HIPAA, she introduced herself and the role she was responsible for in terms of our communication regarding any COVID-19 concerns. In kind, I responded by expressing my belief that it would be critical for me to control as much as possible on my own and rely on her as a resource only when necessary. I shared with her a quote that I wholeheartedly believe in. It is written by a spiritual writer- Lalah Delia, and reads, "Self-care is how you take your power back."

That first call must have lasted about an hour. Immediately after ending that call, my phone rang again. This time the call was from my second assigned nurse. This nurse was calling from the Managed Care Organization that my primary care doctor worked for. It was not my doctor or anyone from her office. She advised me that she was calling from the Managed Care Case Management Department. The call with this nurse followed the same protocol as the call I had with the first nurse. This call also lasted for about an hour. I shared with her the exact quote that I had shared with the first nurse. Before ending the call, I requested that the two nurses work together to ensure that I received optimal healthcare services. I realized that my stress level would become unbearable if they did not work as a team. Collaborating and copying each other's notes made more sense rather than asking me for redundant information. My goal was to rest as much as possible. Before ending the call, the nurse agreed to coordinate care with the other nurse. We ended the call under the agreement that she would call the first nurse and relay my request for the two of them to work together on their efforts related to my care.

I was in for an annoying surprise when just as I was dozing off for a nap, the phone rang again, and the first nurse called me. She inquired about the information I had just provided to the second nurse. I voiced my concern to her that she would call me again instead of working with the first nurse as a tandem pair. I had to have another lengthy conversation in which I told her about my views on patient empowerment, not clinical intervention. Toward the end of the call, she asked if I needed to speak with a behavioral health specialist. My answer was a resounding no. I told her that the only intervention I needed at that time was for her to honor my request and boundary line and work with the other nurse to ensure that I received top-notch health care. At that point, I ended the call. However, that was not the last time I spoke with her; it was also not the last time she mentioned behavioral health services. This unwanted and annoying call left me feeling drained, and the exhaustion I was feeling began to elevate to a different level. Needing a nap, I closed my eyes and began drifting off into sleep, but the rest I envisioned was short-lived as my phone rang again within minutes.

The next call was from a vendor that the hospital had contacted to assist me in three ways. The first was to find a home health agency that would find a skilled nurse or nursing assistant to provide in-home care. The second was to find a physical therapy provider who would provide in-home therapy services. I was a little bewildered by the physical therapy help that they were trying to find. I silently asked myself why I would need physical therapy if I was isolated in one room. I made a mental note to discuss with the nurses why physical therapy was not needed then. It made more sense to me to table the therapy sessions until I was stronger and could move throughout my home. Third, they were to assist with securing an oxygen provider. I laughed when they mentioned that work was being done to secure an oxygen provider. I already had an oxygen provider. I would not have been discharged home without oxygen. I silently asked myself why this vendor was trying to provide me with something I already had. It was clear from the conversation that I was having with this representative that information sharing among vendors was not happening. I ended the call knowing that the road to recovery would be challenging if I did not become an empowered patient.

The vendor representative also did not know that before leaving the hospital, the doctor and the discharge nurse had advised me that it was a long shot but that they would place an order for me to begin in-home nursing care. The doctor provided me with a clinical explanation of the reason for his thoughts, but what I took from what he stated was that because there was no scientific data indicating how the virus was spread that it would be hard to find someone who would be willing to take the chance and come out to visit. Thus, I was skeptical when the vendor called and stated that they had found an agent willing to provide the services. Yet, I listened as the representative told me she would call me back in two hours with more information regarding the nursing agency providing the services. I gave her a sincere thank you before hanging up the phone, so I could sleep. I had no idea that getting some rest was not in the cards. At least not for a while. A different customer service representative from this vendor called me no less than every half an hour that day with the same promise that they knew of a nursing agency that would provide the ordered services. For each initial call that was placed, I would receive a follow-up call stating that they could not find a provider to fulfill the order. It was around 4 p.m. when I finally had enough of taking catnaps and advised the last customer service rep to place a note in the system for no further calls to be made to me until a nursing agency was ready to provide the services. I did not hear from the vendor or the nurses again the rest of the day. Finally, I was able to rest. I did not realize that this cycle of receiving numerous calls from the vendor, all with a promise to find a provider and then with a follow-up call stating one could not be secured, would be repeated day after day until I put a permanent end to it.

Antagonizing as the calls were, I knew that I was one of the lucky ones. I had the ability to speak up and voice my concerns regarding the lack of communication between the clinical team and the vendors. I was also able to speak loud enough for the vendors to understand that they were not to call me, no matter what the issue was. I presented clear instructions on what they should do and how they were expected to do what they must to figure things out before they called me directly.

Foolishness was what was occurring. Foolishness is not to make the patient better; it is the bureaucratic nuisance of the financial priority a hospital has prioritized over patient well-being. In other words, their main concern is to ensure that the insurance company pays them to complete an assigned task.

Sadly, this is routine with a patient when they are discharged from the hospital. The orders from the discharging provider must be completed, but no one calls the patient to see if they have any thoughts on how the orders should be conducted. There may be specific reasons why the patient is left out of the conversation regarding how the orders should be completed, but my argument is that the patient should at least be asked how. Making decisions for the patient without patient input is one of the focal points of non-compliance.

Empowerment of patients in taking a central part in the medical process is done through the encouragement of being savvy medical consumers. Medical consumerism is defined as the idea of the patient taking responsibility by collaborating with their medical team for the medical direction of their personal healthcare journey.

DIARY ENTRY:DAY 12

April 7, 2020. Gasping for air is how I woke up this morning. It feels like someone has reached into my chest walls and removed the entirety of my lungs. I am not sure what is causing this breathing problem, but I am guessing that it has to do with my unease at the use of this oxygen tubing. I have been a total wreck since they inserted the tubing, but when I was in the hospital, I had assistance when it twisted. I am at home now without any assistance, and I am having the darndest time getting acquainted with the apparatus. I will take the time to look at one or two YouTube videos to see how to set the tubing so I can use it easily. I cannot even muster up enough air to try and call my husband. Not that he can come into the room to help me, but he would be able to call someone who can then call me. Shoot! I am hyperventilating as I think of ways to regain proper breathing. This problem was worse at night while I tried to sleep. The previous night was no different. I must have gotten about two hours of actual sleep before I began the night trek of tossing and turning into various positions as I tried to get comfortable.

It was about seven in the morning when my phone rang. It was the first of many calls that I would get from the vendor that day. I would not answer all the calls, but I answered enough to know where the customer service representatives were calling from. I was able to tell that these calls were coming from a different part of the country, and not one of them was reading the notes in the system. One of the representatives even told me that I should begin thinking about admission into a nursing home if they could not locate a nurse willing to provide in-home care. Before ending the call, the representative stated she would continue to find a nursing home agency ready to come into the home. I practically pleaded with her to enter notes into the system that indicated that she was working on my case. I already knew the outcome, although I did not tell her. I was at the point where I could not take one more call from this agency about the fulfillment of an order that I knew was not going to happen. After I received another call from this agency within the hour, I could tell that it was going to take an intervention from a higher force that would stop these customer service representatives from calling me. Thus, I prayed to God that I react to this persistence humbly. I knew these calls were being placed because of one of the many policies for the representatives to follow, but I also knew I would not recover if I could not completely rest.

In addition to gasping for air, I was also irritated from lack of sleep. Reasons for my inability to sleep included experiencing a bad case of heartburn, being short of breath, and being constipated. The last thing I wanted or needed was to receive another annoying call from the vendor. Therefore, I called one of my assigned nurses and requested that they speak to the vendor's office's powers to ensure that my name was placed on the "do not call list." I asked that the vendor be informed that they should relay the information to the nurse, who would then pass along the information to me if communication was needed. I reminded the nurse of my need to rest to regain the strength I needed to overcome the challenges that I was facing. I had no plans to continue the charade with the vendor. I needed to rest to pull my whole body through the challenges brought on by the virus. I shared with the nurse my concern that I would not be successful if I received a call from the vendor's office every half hour. We all knew that the successful completion of the order was not going to be made. I received one final call from the vendor before my "do not call" request was acknowledged. That last call, which initially appeared hopeful, turned out to be yet another snafu before the day was over.

An overarching problem with the current healthcare system is that finding good medical assistance can be equated to finding a needle in a haystack. It is a rarity for a patient to get the help they need in accessing medical resources on the first call to either a provider's office, a vendor's office, or the insurance company. It is important to remember that it is not the fault of the person that the patient is talking to on the phone does not know all the specifics about the policies and procedures that are put into place by the executives that oversee that specific office.

Corporate and medical executive leaders are not the same people on the front lines answering the calls that are being placed by people desperately in need of services. These also are not the same people who feel the need to fully train their staff on how to correctly offer A+ medical assistance to patients who are often at their wit's end in trying to obtain medical resources and services needed to promote self-care and full healing. These are, however, the same bigwigs that have no problem passing the patient around like a hot potato while trying to avoid offering helpful assistance to those in need. There are ways to avoid being caught in the trap of endlessly searching for what should be forthcoming questions. Using the voice as a tool is one way to guarantee an optimal level of medical assistance. Speaking up is vitally important. Closed mouths do not get fed nor receive the type of assistance so often needed.

Speaking loudly is a second way to get the medical assistance needed without getting frustrated and throwing up your hands. During my public speaking engagements and when I speak to my clients, I tell them that speaking loud does not mean being egotistical or boastful. It means talking with a sass when your request for the right medical assistance is not offered. There are always two or more ways to skin a cat. Speaking loudly can be done vocally and in writing. Become a pro at using tools such as Twitter and grievance letters to bring attention to receiving inadequate medical assistance. Speak Often! Repeating a request for medical assistance over and over may be what is needed to obtain medical assistance. You may get tired, and your voice may weaken from repetitive talking, but that is okay just do not relinquish your power and your right to receive unparalleled medical assistance. In addition, there are other ways to get medical assistance, but the three ways are sure-proof ways to receive remarkable medical assistance.

DIARY ENTRY:DAY 13

April 8, 2020. Still struggling is how I woke up this morning, Woozy and out of sorts for yet another day. I have the same feeling that I had on the previous day, only triple the intensity. I will contact both of my assigned nurses, and hopefully, one of them will promptly call me back to discuss the symptoms that I am having. To ensure that I speak to someone who can advise me on why I am experiencing a bad case of heartburn combined with constipation, I will call my insurance company's 24/7 nurse line. The nurse who answers may be able to make suggestions on things to try for alleviation purposes.

Hopefully, the remainder of the day will be uneventful. I am in such bad shape that I want to lie down. I am in so much pain that all I want to do is sleep. If that does not work, I will resort to watching television. I am becoming unfairly angry with myself for the condition I am in. I am now questioning why God is allowing me to be in so much pain.

Yesterday, my older sister called me, and when I told her what a rotten day I had, she spoke reality to me when she said to me that the pain would not always last and that the worse would soon be over. She said, "hang in there, Sis; don't you dare give up." Since I am no quitter, I decided to fight through the remainder of the evening.

DIARY ENTRY:DAY 14

April 9, 2020. Alas, Rest arrives. I woke up this morning as if the tired and weary body that I had grown I had grown accustomed to had reached a plateau, and the tide was beginning to turn. The restlessness that I had suffered through since being discharged from the hospital had gotten better, and I was able to sleep. The relentless calls that I was getting from the clinical team and vendors had slowed to a snail's pace. Serenity and peace are within reach, but I am still experiencing challenges. The heartburn had dissipated but was not completely gone. I was still having a problem making a bowel movement without straining, so I ate as little as possible. In addition, Good Friday and Easter were coming, and I was hoping that I would have the good fortune of being blessed with my mother-in-law's home-cooked holiday meal, which consisted of turkey and dressing. I owed it to myself to veer off the course of eating from a bland diet; , my body was wreaking havoc on me. I told myself that drinking Ensure was a better choice for me today. It was a nutritious sweet drink, not a bland blah-blah drink. I was not concerned at all that the Glucerna was the preferred drink of choice.

The solace that day came from listening to church services that had recently begun broadcasting via the Internet and listening to gospel music. Doing these two activities helped calm my soul and soothe my fears when I started to contemplate just how much longer I would have to deal with the agonizing gastrointestinal and digestive symptoms I was experiencing.

Listening in solitude gave me time to reflect on all I had been through since the beginning of this year. Yes, I had been through challenges, but I was blessed to be alive. There were a lot of people who did not make it. I also took advantage of the quiet of the day to make plans for the coming week. I had goals that I wanted to achieve. I was determined to complete these goals in the upcoming week. There was one thing that I had to do before I could do anything else, and as soon as possible, I would be completing that task on Friday morning. It was of high importance that I speak to one or both of my assigned nurses about gastrointestinal and digestive problems. Real relief was needed. The level of pain that I was having was unbearable.

Post Discharge Planning is a process in which the clinical team meets with the patient and the patient's support team. This support team consists of family, friends, and sometimes a paid advocate, all of whom will be readily available if the patient needs assistance during recovery. During this meeting, the medical provider discusses self-management practices for the patient to follow once they are discharged from the hospital. Information regarding what to expect during the home healing process, side effects from medication, symptoms that may indicate the need for a return to the hospital, and when follow-up appointments should be scheduled are just key points discussed during the meeting. It is imperative for the patient to speak up and add his/her voice to the discharge planning conversation. Preparing a list and sharing it with the support team just in case they are unable to speak helps to ensure that the patient's concerns are fully addressed and that the answers provided by the medical team are explained and understood.

DIARY ENTRY:DAY 15

April 10, 2020. TGIF! It is Friday. This day could not come fast enough. I must speak to one or both of my assigned nurses. Hopefully, one of them will answer the phone when I call this morning.

I reach for my cell phone and call one nurse. She does not answer, so I leave her a message to call me back and hang up to call the other nurse. That nurse was available, and she had time to speak with me. She listened empathetically as I told her about the intensified pain I was experiencing. When I was through with sharing my concerns, she shared with me clinical information on why I was experiencing the symptoms that were present. According to the nurse,

the gastrointestinal and digestive symptoms problems that I was having were due to my body shutting completely down while I was in the hospital. The nurse used an interactive approach to solve the dilemma regarding what was causing the pain. I had grown angry with myself for not rebounding as quickly as I thought I would when I was discharged from the hospital. Two questions were all that was needed to solve the dilemma and release the anger. They both said I could call them if I needed to talk or had any questions. I am eager to speak with at least one of them. I needed an unequivocal explanation for why I was still in so much pain. The second question she asked was: When was the last time I exercised for at least thirty minutes? After providing my answer to her, she asked me to take moments to reflect on my answers. Once I took the time to think about my responses, it was easy to understand the clinical information she provided to me. According to her explanation, the problems I was experiencing could be attributed to my body has shut down quite a bit since I first became ill. She used the old rusty wheel story as an example of what was occurring within my body. She advised me that just like the old rusty wheel, it needs to be lubricated before it can get back into gear. I was informed that the symptoms would get better once I was able to move around more. Additionally, the nurse advised me that soft and bland foods would be beneficial in alleviating e of the discomforts I was experiencing. Together we planned a diet that included bland foods like mashed potatoes, yogurt, bananas, and strained vegetables. Before we ended our conversation, she reminded me that slow and steady wins the race.

After ending the call with the nurse, my friend called. That call reminded me that God's grace on me included blessing me with the people who make up my circle of life. If it were not for these incredibly special people, I am not sure what the outcome would have been for me. These are people whom I consider to be good and faithful friends. They seemed always to have known when they were needed, even without me saying a word to them. My mother has raised me to understand good and faithful friends are hard to find. I was raised on my mother's words of wisdom that a good friend is hard to find and that when I find a good friend, I should value that friendship and hold onto it for dear life. This lesson has been brought to life as I have progressed through this virus. My circle of friends is truly remarkable. They pray with me and for me as I continue battling this virus. They call, text, and encourage me to rest and regain my strength. Thus, when my friend called and, after praying with me, invited me to her church's virtual Good Friday service and offered to bring me some Palms and Sacramental wine and crackers to partake in, the spiritual Good Friday Service, I was overcome with joy.

My heart is swelling with the thought that I will be able to participate in a solemn Good Friday spiritual service. Within the hour of our call ending, my friend texted me to tell me that she had sat the Palms and the Sacramental offerings outside on my porch. My husband went and retrieved them. I sensed humility and thankfulness when I looked at the Palms. I have hung the Palms in my room, and for the remainder of the day, I have remained excited and anxious with anticipation for the spiritual service that I will be able to take part in that evening. The service was just what I needed. It left me with a sense of tranquility. I should be able to sleep tonight like a newborn baby with no care in this world.

Patient autonomy also referred to as the patient's right to choose, provides legal power to patients who are of sound mind and body the right to choose what clinical guidance they will adhere to reach optimal health outcomes. Sadly, patients often choose to exercise this option to self-heal when they have difficulty finding a medical provider and their level of pain has reached an excruciating level that, without giving a second thought to the involved risk they turn to self-medicating processes.

DIARY ENTRY:DAY 16

April 11, 2020. It is the dawn of a new day. I am continuing to heal, and after the conversation, I had with the nurse yesterday, I decided to begin to wean myself off the oxygen. I still need to use it somewhat, but I am sure that I no longer need to use it twenty-four hours a day. I also feel that my all-day use of oxygen contributes to the longevity of my gastrointestinal and digestive problems. As a result, I have decided to use oxygen only at night because I have noticed that my breathing becomes labored if I do not. I have been feeling out of sorts for the past few days. My husband has been urging me to drink a glass of Prune Juice to see if that will help. Yesterday, I begrudgingly listened to him and had him pour me a glass. Surprisingly instead of sipping on the drink, I closed my eyes and imagined that the cup I was drinking from was a nice tall glass of ice water on a sweltering summer day. It did not immediately help, so being impatient, I took a stool softener about two hours after I drank the prune juice. That was one of the worse decisions I could have ever made. As a result of taking that combination, my stool has become even harder than it was before. I have spent a lot of time since then in bed, tossing and turning from the pain I unnecessarily put myself through. I made a promise to myself that I will never, ever do that again.

Consuming food is something that we all do. Maintaining and balancing a healthy diet by eating nutritious foods is a definite must for everyone. Reintroducing a vitamin-enriched diet to a patient who has lost an extreme amount of water weight due to an illness is not an easy task, but; it is a process that should be encouraged. I opine that discussing and then preparing a self-management diet with a Registered

Dietitian, a meal expert who has met academic and professional requirements, should become a standard part of the discharge planning process.

DIARY ENTRY: DAY 17

April 12, 2020. Alas, Easter Sunday has arrived. I am in a somber mood. Surprisingly, I am hungry. Salivating, my mind is visualizing a home-cooked meal. Securing a home-cooked meal is my goal for today. Light eating for me this morning will be a turkey sausage link, a hash brown potato patty, and a glass of orange juice. I am determined that nothing will stand in my way of enjoying a healthy home-cooked meal should one be offered. Hopefully, the light breakfast will keep me full until lunchtime. Prayerfully, by then, I will have additional options to choose from. Currently, the two choices that will be available are to order from a restaurant or have someone bring me a plate of home-cooked food. I have my fingers crossed that the latter will win out and that my mother-in-law will send one of her delicious home-cooked meals.

My doorbell has been rung. The angels have arrived at the door. My home-cooked meal has arrived. I am not sure if it was greed or a desire for a home-cooked meal that drove my effort to eat as much of the food as possible, but whatever it was, I tried my hardest. I soon found out that all the action was for naught.

Research shows at least four key benefits to Autobiographical Story Telling, the process of sharing the storytellers' personal experiences, which have created a memorable experience they want to share with others. As it relates to healthcare, there is one specific benefit that has a direct correlation to the healing process for both the healing patient and the healed patient. I opine that the storyteller offers a balm of Gilead type of healing through sharing their story. Drawing the reader or listener into a story regarding how they were at their lowest level of despair and were encouraged through that lonely period by a memorable experience that helped them heal. Hearing stories of this magnitude has the potential for the healer to reflect upon their own experiences and continue to fight through the illness.

DIARY ENTRY: DAY 18

April 13, 2020. Writhing in pain is how I awoke this morning. I have never felt this kind of pain before. Last night was horrible. I spent the entire evening writhing in pain until about 12:30 am before finally falling fast asleep. It is now one in the afternoon. I might have slept longer if my husband, who had not grown concerned, woke me up to ensure I was okay. He had brought me breakfast, and I had not even acknowledged the breakfast tray was in my room. Then when lunchtime came around, and I still had not arisen, he became even more worried.

I am fully awake now. I will try to eat as much lunch as I can once I have cleared the cobwebs from my eyes. I will then have a heart-to-heart talk with my husband. So that he is made fully aware of what I am experiencing, I will tell him of the level of pain and misery with which I am dealing. Since bedrooms still separated us, he could only hear my pain; he could not physically see exactly what was occurring. He will ask me if there is anything he can do to make things better. I am sure he is already praying for my full healing, but we must bring this issue to God.

As we began praying for each other and our married life, a new vigor was birthed into me to fight as hard as I could to overcome the challenges with which I was faced. I am holding myself accountable from this day forward to think with an optimistic mindset that everything would be ok if I would hold on. As we ended our talk, I vividly remembered how when I was a little girl, my grandmother used to hum and sing the words written by John Newton in the hymnal of Amazing Grace, and I clung to the words that spoke to the situation I was now in.

The remainder of that day was uneventful. I experienced a sense of serenity and peace. It was like a calm had come over me. This brought to my mind a scripture found in Mark 4:39 (KJV), which says, Jesus rebukes the wind and tells the sea, "Peace be still," and the wind stopped blowing, and there was a great calm.

Shared Decision Making is a Model of Care that encourages the medical provider and patient's collaboration in developing a Plan of Care wherein both the clinician and patient are encouraged to learn from each other. In this manner, a joint decision is made on the options available to the patient that will result in the patient receiving optimal health care services. In addition to each side learning from the other, the physician and the patient have an opportunity to explain their differences and similarities in the thought process. The open line of communication between the medical team and the patient that is encouraged with the use of the Shared Decision Model often results in the patient receiving the best health outcomes available. This Model of Care allows for the patient's voice to be included in the self-management process. As such this Model of Care provides the patient with the empowerment tools needed to become their own patient advocate.

DIARY ENTRY: DAY 19

Today is April 14, 2020. Yesterday, I promised myself that I would start each day with a positive affirmation. Today's affirmation is that I will have a formidable day. Last week, I received approval from my doctor that I no longer needed to be self-isolated. This, of course, depended on my ability to be fever-free for three days without medication. We jointly agreed that my moving about would be a good jump-start point for regaining my strength. When I woke up this morning, I managed to gather enough vim and vigor to attempt, with the assistance of my husband, to walk to the end of the block. I figured walking to the block's end would make for a manageable walk.

While I am getting dressed, I hear what sounds like the pitter-patter of raindrops outside my window. I become a little bit dismayed, but it is still early enough that there is a good chance that the weather will clear up a little later. I have been locked away from the real world for over three months. I turn on the news, and my heart sinks a little further when the weather reporter forecasts rain for the remainder of the week. Great! another monkey wrench is being thrown into my plan. Be patient, I tell myself. You will be walking outside in the sunshine and warmth soon.

Now that my plans have been squashed for the day, I decide to put on my superwoman cape and venture into the basement to do laundry. First, I must wait for my husband to take his daily nap as I am sure under no terms is he going to go along with the foolishness of my attempt to complete laundry. Once I know that he is asleep, I will proceed with my plan to wash a load of laundry.

Once I was sure he was asleep, I proceeded to what turned out to be a fool-hearted decision. It must have taken me about ten minutes to make it down the eight stairs leading to my laundry room. It took all my strength to put one foot in front of the other to make it to the laundry room. I stood in my laundry room, unsure of how I would gain the strength needed to make it back upstairs to my living room. Each step I took going back up the stairs tired me out even more. As soon as I made it to the last stage and took that final breath, I headed toward the living room. I was hoping that my husband was still asleep, but there he was, wide awake, sitting on the couch, with a look of discernment. He wanted to know what the rush was that I had to do laundry. He was not happy with my attempt to do more than I was supposed to be doing, especially because I did not have to push myself to the point of no return. I did not have an answer to his question of why I felt the need to overexert myself. As he continued to talk, I tried to listen, but my body was so tired that all I wanted was my bed. I spent the rest of the day in bed, too exhausted to do anything but sleep. So much for my walking plan. I hoped it would continue to rain that day. At least then, I would have some consolation about not walking.

DIARY ENTRY: DAY 20

April 15, 2020. Oh no! the pain has returned. I am trying to think of a positive affirmation, but this pain is making it difficult to think positively. This day has certainly started off on a bad note. It feels like someone has taken a match and lit my gastrointestinal system on fire. I have a severe case of indigestion, and my bowel system is blocked. As if that is not bad enough, I am having difficulty urinating. Depression is starting to set in. I begin wondering if this pain will ever end. I have surpassed the seven to fourteen-day infectious period listed on the Centers for Disease Control website. I cannot figure out why this relapse in my symptoms had appeared. To say I am questioning God and why he is allowing this to happen would be an understatement. I am beginning to think that I may need to be re-hospitalized. I begin praying for the strength needed to call one or both of my assigned nurses to find out what could have caused this type of blockage. Last night, I did not sleep well. I try thinking of something that has changed in my daily routine, and nothing comes to mind. I did feast on a wonderful home-cooked meal on Easter Sunday. Surely, that could not be the cause, but I will find out once I speak with the nurse.

I am hungry, but I think it's best that I skip eating breakfast. Instead, I will just drink a glass of prune juice and eat two graham crackers. I will then take a nap. I will call the nurses after I wake up.

It is about 10:00 am when I wake. After washing up and changing into new pajamas, I then had the urge to go to the bathroom. I began to feel hopeful that things would change and that the symptoms would ease up, but after spending close to an hour on the commode straining, I was sure that something horrible was happening. When I finally stood up from the commode, I slowly made it back to my bedroom, where I called the nurses. Each of them phoned me back and asked me if I had done anything differently, and when I responded no, their next question was about what I had eaten over the past few days. I provided them with the foods I had eaten, and neither seemed to be concerned until I mentioned the foods that were a part of my holiday dinner. It was then concluded that the culprit was the Potato Salad and Turkey. According to their responses, the coarseness of the Potatoes and Turkey was causing my digestive/gastrointestinal problems. They both advised me that my system was still not ready for foods that took effort in being digested. I was told that my diet should be bland and liquid until I could get up and move around more. I made a mental note to put effort into taking a walk to the corner before the week was out.

DIARY ENTRY: DAY 21

April 16, 2020. Finally, I am feeling better. Sure, I still had severe indigestion, but it was nowhere near as bad as it had been in the previous few days. I was still trying to figure out what was the cause of indigestion. I have not eaten anything other than soup and graham crackers. I am beginning to question the validity of what the nurses had told me about eating the holiday meal and vowed that I would ask my husband to assist me with walking to the end of the block if the weather held up. To ensure that I was up to the challenge of venturing outside, something I had not done in three months, I decided to relax that day; thus, I spent the day doing nothing but gathering my thoughts and enjoying my hobbies. I watched television, searched the Internet, listened to Gospel music, and talked/texted on my phone.

My meals for the day consisted of soups and juices. Thus, it came as a surprise when indigestion started creeping back in later in the evening. Oh no, I thought, not again. Determined to fight off this dreadful feeling, I quickly started thinking of other remedies that we had at home that I would use before I contracted COVID-19. I remembered that we had a bottle of Pepto Bismol and a box of baking powder at home. I am not sure why I first thought of Pepto Bismol but thank God I did. I was able to venture into my kitchen and quickly took a dose of the Pepto Bismo. Within an hour, my indigestion had subsided, and I was able to rest.

DIARY ENTRY: DAY 22

April 17, 2020. TGIF! I am alert and mentally psyched for the walk I will take today. This is the first time in a long time that I remember waking up unaware of any ailments. I mean, there is no indigestion or bowel issues.

I slept last night with the oxygen cannula on without pulling it out or feeling discomforted with having it on. I am ecstatic. Although, I am silently questioning why neither of my nurses had the forethought to suggest trying Pepto Bismo or something over the counter to alleviate the problems that I was having.

Not one to dwell on the negative. My mind is focused on the words, Self-Help: with this in mind, I now have a fire in me to push past the challenge of walking down the street and rebuilding my strength. The weather is beautiful. I have listened to the newscasters, and none were forecasting rain. Today is going to be an excellent day for walking. After washing up, dressing, and eating breakfast, I will begin my walk.

As I began to move, it seemed like my block had been redesigned, and additional houses had been added. The street was longer than I remembered. I took small steps and made it down the block. About halfway to the end of the block, my mind and body started having an internal fight. My body was saying, stop walking.

Turn around. You are going to fall flat on your face if you take another step. My mind was telling me to keep walking. My mind was telling me that I could do it. My mind was visually recalling those two words: Self. . .Help! I opted to listen to my mind. My husband told me to stop if I could not make it, and we would again the next day, but he also knew that I was persistent and would keep going. I made it through to the end of the block. As I rounded the corner and made my way back to my home, the steps I took began to quicken. It took me less time to reach my home than it did to walk in the opposite direction. I was thankful, grateful, and tired.

Minutes after making it home, I washed my hands, replaced the oxygen cannula, went to bed, and took a nap. My mind had won the overall challenge, but my body had the last say. I slept like a baby this afternoon with not care in the world. I woke up at about four o'clock in the afternoon. Ready to take on another walk and an even longer walk on the following day. The remainder of the day was uneventful. I even ate a full meal for dinner. I felt confident that indigestion would not arise, and if it did, I would take the Pepto Bismo as soon as I felt it creeping in.

Two factors are extremely helpful to a patient's healing process. One factor is that the patient remains encouraged and does not fall into a mindset of despair. Yes, there will be days that are rougher than others, but they must continue to fight through those challenging days. The second factor is that a strong external support network of friends and family should be readily available to give the patient the strength to overcome those challenges.

A dedicated support network can serve as an advocate for the patient until they regain their strength. That advocacy is needed not only to speak on the patient's behalf but they can also offer an empathetic ear to encourage a patient through the challenges they face on a difficult day.

DIARY ENTRY: DAY 23

April 18, 2020, well, another weekend on the road to recovery. I was awoken by my phone ringing. It was my oldest sister who was calling to check in on me. We had not spoken in what must have been two days, which was unusual for us as the one daily constant I depended on was receiving a call or a text from her. It felt strange not to have spoken to her in a few days because she was my one constant reminder that God was carrying me through this process. I felt much better after she assured me that she received daily updates from my other sister, mother, and husband. They must have shared the pain and weakness that they heard in my voice with her. I opine that knowing this, she decided it was best to pray from afar for me to gain my strength.

When we spoke, she advised me that she had spoken to my husband the prior evening, and he had told her that it would be ok to call me. I told her that, yes, I had been having rough days. They were getting better. I told her about the relief I received from taking the Pepto Bismo. She was glad to hear that I was rebounding but encouraged me to continue to take the baby steps needed to heal completely. When we ended the call, it was time to prepare for the remainder of the day. After showering and eating breakfast, I watched television and listened to gospel music. Then I took a short nap.

When I woke up, my husband asked me what I wanted for lunch. Before answering his question, I thought about how much it would cost if I wanted something we did not have in the house. I was so used to going to a restaurant whenever I wanted and making up my mind while I was in the store on what I wanted. Thanks to the virus, that process had changed. I had to depend on others. My friends and family were available and helped me when they could by either cooking a meal, offering to cook a meal, or going to pick up what I wanted. Of course, they did not charge me; however, if there was something special I wanted or did not want to bother them. I would have to rely on delivery services such as Uber Eats, Door Dash, Grub Hub, or the restaurant I wanted something from. Choosing to use a delivery service was not free. There was a delivery charge attached to using their services. It was understandable that there was a fee involved with having items delivered, but there seemed to be an upcharge engaged in food delivery. I decided against having food delivered and settled for a frozen dinner readily available in our freezer.

Having an external support network that constantly stands in the gap for a patient and makes themselves readily available through not only their words, but their actions relieve the stress and worries that often saddle the patient recovering from a debilitating illness. Such a network allows the patient to concentrate on healing and not on any other mitigating issues that may impede the healing process. I was thankful that I was blessed with family and friends who cared enough to be an active part of my support network by either calling, texting, and sending words of encouragement but also acting in the same accord.

DIARY ENTRY: DAY 24

April 20, 2020. Sunday is a day of rest and reflection. It is also my favorite day of the week. I woke up today praying for another uneventful day. My agenda for the day will include spending time reflecting on my life, listening to Gospel music, and listening to various media channels on how this virus is devastating minority communities. I have every intent on keeping the promise I made to myself to get better so that I could be a positive influence in my community on ways to minimize the devastation. First, I had to keep pushing myself, which meant planning to go for another walk in the coming days and encouraging myself to begin driving my car again.

DIARY ENTRY: DAY 25

April 21, 2020. The start of another work week and I am up and energized. Shockingly, I am feeling like I am a new person. I am starting to think that the worst may be over. I slept peacefully last evening. I had not a care in the world, or at least that is what I thought. I prepared myself for another morning walk. After eating breakfast, I began walking. My steps were not as slow as the previous day. I had a pep in my step. I was gaining so much confidence that I walked to and from the corner twice before my body told me to stop. After the walk, I did not immediately need to take a nap. For once, I had energy. I began looking forward to the Post Corona days and what positive changes I would incorporate into my everyday life. I looked forward to giving praise and testimony for what God had brought me to and through. I realized that life could be snatched away from you within a blink of an eye.

I decided to make another move that would help my healing process. I planned to discontinue the use of my oxygen. I had not been given any instructions on how long I needed to keep the oxygen on. Since I was already on the minimum dosage of oxygen, now would be a perfect time to discontinue the usage entirely. I had a challenging time reaching my primary care doctor to inquire about stopping the oxygen. Neither of my two nurses answered clearly when I should stop using the oxygen tank. Thus, I was provided with no clinical direction.

I spoke with one of my sisters, who encouraged me to keep it on when I went to bed, so for a few days, I did just that.

DIARY ENTRY: DAY 26

April 22, 2020. Decreasing the oxygen on the prior day provided me with a deep sense of relief. It is Tuesday now, and for the first time in a long time, I can breathe without gasping for air, and my indigestion seems to have dissipated.

The last couple of months have been physically and mentally draining for me. So, I am thankful that the worse days are behind me. Relaxing and Rejuvenating is how I will spend this week. I am moving away from being so harsh on myself for not recuperating as quickly as I normally would when I am sick. Starting with today and moving forward, I will do all I can to ensure that I take every moment every day to breathe and breathe out the fullness of life. One thing I have learned from dealing with the effects of COVID-19 is that it is critical not to overwhelm myself by putting too many tasks on my to-do list. I am thankful that I am on the road to full recovery.

DIARY ENTRY: DAY 27

April 23, 2020. Today is Wednesday, and I hope that I will be able to have the same type of restful day that I had yesterday. Relaxing and Rejuvenating is how I spent the day yesterday. Today I am looking forward to doing much of what I did yesterday. I will also begin reconnecting with the people I have lost contact with. I make a mental note to not overdue the verbal communication part. Tiring myself out is not the goal. Thus, limiting myself to no more than three vocal calls of no more than 30 minutes each with unlimited texting will be my mode of Operandi for the day. Getting to this point in my recovery period was something I was getting used to, and I was enjoying life again.

DIARY ENTRY: DAY 28

April 24, 2020. It is Thursday, or as I call it, Friday Eve. Funny thing, I was so busy pampering myself that I totally missed the clues that the easy, carefree days were a precursor for the rough days that would soon follow. I have spent an inordinate amount of time over the last few days focusing as much of my attention as I can on doing the things I want to do rather than the ones I must do.

CHAPTER 4

HEALTHCARE FINANCES FOR THE PATIENT

*"Capitalism is a social system
owned by the capitalist class, a
small network of very wealthy
and powerful businessmen,
who compromise the health
and security of the general
population for corporate gain."*

*— Suzy Kassem, Rise Up and
Salute the Sun: The Writings of
Suzy Kassem*

Alas, the month of May had arrived. It had been a month that I had been looking forward to. I have spent the previous few months in a state of constant healing. From all accounts, the healing process should have been over two months ago, yet here I was at what I thought was the end. Finally, I would have the time to reflect on the economic disarray caused by this virus within the minority, women, and impoverished communities.

I noticed one issue that I had not heard discussed on any of the social media postings or daily press briefings. This one issue kept consistently being repeated. The more it came up, the less I felt like a human being and more like an object with a money tag attached.

With each passing day, I saw how business marketing firms targeted another healthcare issue to increase the profit margin from red to black. It was clear to me that COVID was becoming a 'cash cow," otherwise known as an economic opportunity for the business community. As a health policy administrator student, I studied the impact of how Socioeconomic dynamics impacted the lives of those living in the communities that were most negatively impacted by the start of the pandemic. The one commonality that was present in all the past pandemics and from the information being broadcasted about COVID-19 was that the communities that could least afford to be negatively impacted were the ones that were hit the hardest and suffered the most as it related to economic damage. Surreal is the picture that was painted in the textbooks. I remember constantly thinking about how people could live through the tough times that were thrust upon them. Fear, the uncertainty of the future, public disgrace, and the loss of life of friends and family were just three of the social factors that people living in what is referred to as disparaging communities or considered to be a minority, whether it was based on color, gender or age were forced to live through in each of the pre-pandemic. Add to this the economic strain due to job loss or health status that was forced on these communities.

Pure dismay and dishevelment are what people living in these communities had to fight against. My heart sank, and I prayed that I would never live to see another upheaval in those communities. Yet here I was, reading, watching, and participating in another disruption. The goal was to heal fully, but in pursuing that goal, I had to help with the process of price gouging and profit raising that I was getting drawn into.

During the second week of May, I decided to compose a list of items that would be helpful in my ongoing health process and for those who were impacted by COVID-19 or had friends and loved ones who were. Heck! It was a sound economic investment. Prices were already on the rise for all necessities, and the second wave of COVID-19 was predicted. It was being forecasted to arrive during the fall and winter seasons when those who did not have ready access to transportation would have a tough time getting transported to stores to purchase items, and those who were cash-strapped would have a challenging time getting access to needed items. Countless media outlets were reporting on price gouging that was going on across the country, and I was hearing first-hand accounts of the price gouging that was going on in marginalized communities.

My list included a calculation, comparison, and availability chart of the items needed when recovering from a debilitating or chronic condition. I had an idea of the results but was shocked to see both the gap in consumer usage and the increase in cost over the prior year.

As I looked at what I thought was a completed list, I noticed that it was not complete. It lacked a crucial shipping column. This column was required because some stores were closed, and many of the items would have to be shipped. This raised another possibility: either people, including myself, would learn how to be creative in creating do-it-yourself kits, or we would contribute to the profit margin of shipping companies and pay to have the essentials delivered. I also noticed that it would be more time-efficient for me to separate the items into shopping categories. Since I was having memory issues, this helped me determine if my list included everything I needed, not just items I wanted. As I looked at the fully compiled list, a couple of things immediately came to mind. First, I was reminded how blessed I was. God had given my husband and me the foresight to stockpile vital products needed in an emergency. I was grateful that we were provided with the means to save for these items and thought it would be helpful that everyone is aware of these items so that they could begin to stockpile these items for times like those presented during the COVID pandemic, which comes unannounced. I must admit that when we were saving these items, they appeared to me to be small meaningless items, but due to the virus, I now viewed them as worthy commodities that everyone should have at their disposal.

I also noticed that during my illness and throughout my healing process, I had not been paying close attention to how the focus had moved from human empathy to economic wealth. I was now at a time of reflection and peace. Thus, I was able to see a clearer picture of everyday occurrences. So, it was no surprise that I began to see that money had been a primary force from the moment I was diagnosed as positive. I began to subconsciously think about two occurrences that happened in the weeks since I had been discharged from the hospital. These two occurrences caused me to conclude that money and not empathy for human life had been the primary focus since news of the Coronavirus had been publicized. The first of the two occurrences started the moment I entered the hospital. I could visually see the wheels of money turning. I began wondering how I missed the money signs, which are now the focus of yet another pandemic. The thought that I had become a pawn in the money game depressed me. That feeling did not last long as I realized that I had to focus on how to limit the Coronavirus's monetary impact on me and the communities in which I belonged and how to pass that information along to others, especially those who could least afford it.

I then began thinking about that first conversation with the vendor who was entrusted to seek nursing services and an oxygen provider for me. It was not until I took a closer look at the conversation I had with the vendor, who was more focused on admitting me into a skilled nursing facility than providing me with the option of self-monitoring. The vendor's argument at the time was that I would not be held financially liable for the stay because any COVID-19 medical services rendered would be paid in full by my insurance company. I could see that no one was truly listening to my concern that the premiums being deducted from my husband's paycheck for medical insurance partially funded any medical services I received. Additionally, no one seemed to know or care that once the Corona Virus dust had settled and life was back to normal, I, as a patient, may have to pay a higher deductible. I thought that all this so-called free medical care being offered to every-one would eventually have to be paid for.

Another matter directly connected to the high deductible issue is that, like everything else, the taxpayer would be responsible for the cost, and as a taxpayer, I wanted to ensure that my contribution was being used for my benefit.

CHAPTER 5

HOW TO BALANCE A HEALTHY BODY AND A HEALTHY POCKET: THE RELATIONSHIP BETWEEN HEALTH AND THE ECONOMY

*The rich and the poor have this in
common. The LORD is the maker
of them all. (
-Proverbs 22:2) (KJV)*

Media reports regarding the number of people who have been diagnosed with chronic medical conditions such as Diabetes, Hypertension, COPD, Asthma, and now COVID-19 appear to focus on the famous and not the destitute. I opine that this does two things. First, it draws attention to healthcare inequities. The differences in services provided are transparent. Many news outlets reported a shortage of testing supplies for COVID-19. These same reports discussed how the rich and famous were being assessed numerous times. Secondly, it causes outrage in the economically and downtrodden communities. People were rightfully upset. They were voicing complaints on how they were unable to be tested one time when others were tested multiple times. People with money were able to buy medicine and healthcare services. People without money had to wait. This was not right, but it was the truth. This was just one side of the Rich Man/Poor Man social saga that I, along with others, got trapped into with our positive diagnosis, but it was not the first time, and it certainly would not be the last time that the difference between the rich and poor would be a central focus of a healthcare issue.

It is a well-known fact that inequality in healthcare between the rich and poor, the white and the brown, has been a social problem for decades. The presence of COVID-19 and the consistent barrage of written news reports and media photo ops helped fuel the fire that the gaps that were present in past Pandemics and Epidemics related to the rich and poor, the white and brown are still present. This is unfortunate because the type of coverage that was being publicized fueled anger in those communities that could least afford it. Resources should have been available for all but were only provided to a chosen few. Hospitals in very challenged neighborhoods reported a lack of PPE equipment and masks intended to keep the clinical team workers and patients safe from infections. In contrast, little was reported about those issues in affluent communities. Clearly, the Socioeconomic issues of past pandemics and epidemics were once again on the rise.

The inequitable distribution of equipment to treat and keep patients, their loved ones, and their community safe from contracting this horrendous virus that was killing thousands of people daily was being reported. A more sustainable health equity law is needed. The policies and procedures written into that law must be used to implement positive change. Maybe then the social woes experienced by those who are already wantonly suffering will receive the correct attention.

CHAPTER 6

A SURVIVAL GUIDE FOR PATIENTS

*"I fight for my health every day
in ways that most people don't
understand. I'm not lazy. I'm a
warrior!"*
– Unknown.

Amid studying the economic and social impact of the myriad of chronic medical conditions on the marginalized communities that I belong to, my body started reexhibiting symptoms and signs associated with the residual effects of COVID-19. My body took on a whole new dimension.

DIARY ENTRY: DAY 31

May 20, 2020. An itching sensation is what awoke me this morning. I noticed two .

minor rashes starting to form—one on my arm and one on my leg. Additionally, my vaginal area was beginning to itch severely. Other than the rash spreading and getting redder, I didn't have any other problems. I had no idea what was causing the inflammation and the itching. My primary care doctor is not in her office, so my calls to the customer service unit will probably not be responded to. The chances are high that the pain will linger. I really am not up to going to the emergency room. Since I have no fever, they will just send me home. Truth be told, I am fearful that they will find another reason to admit me, and mentally I am prepared to be readmitted to the hospital.

In the past, home remedies helped. I am going to look to see what I think will alleviate the symptoms I am experiencing. Shoot! I look, but I cannot find anything, and this itching is getting to be unbearable. I will have to ask my husband to drive me to the pharmacy. I need something to try and keep the rash and itching under control. If I do not get something immediately, I am afraid of the outcome. I have not started driving myself, and I am afraid that I may get into an accident if I try driving myself. The itching is excruciating.

We made it to the pharmacy, and I jump out of the car and walk as quickly as possible to the aisle where I thought I would find relief. I did not realize I had made a mistake until much later. I found a box of extra strength Vagisil. This purchase gave me a false sense of hope. I was confident that it would relieve the itching, and it did for a brief time. It gave me the relief I needed to sleep. It was not long before I woke up in excruciating pain.

The rash had spread to other areas of my body, and the itching had intensified. Again, I had to rely on the 24-hour nurse line to determine what to do and why this was happening. I told the nurse about the symptoms I was experiencing, and she told me that I was allergic to Vagisil. She provided me with two options: to either proceed to the Emergency Room or take Benadryl. Great! I thought just what I needed, another setback. I wondered when or if this madness would ever end. Since it was already late in the evening, I opted to take Benadryl after my husband returned from the pharmacy. I promised myself that I would find a medical provider who would be open the following day to be examined and that could correctly diagnose me with what was causing the itching.

What a day! Just when I thought that I was past the healing mark. A depressing point for sure. Quizzically, I wonder why absolutely no one prepared me for what to fully expect once I was discharged. I knew the healing process would not be a walk in the park; in no way did I think I would still be having the challenges and issues that kept populating. Yet here I was, still dealing with the ramifications of this virus attacking my system.

DIARY ENTRY: DAY 32

May 21, 2020. It is the dawning of a new day! Last night after taking the Benadryl, I was able to sleep. Once I get myself together and eat breakfast, I will call my insurance company to find a provider office that is open. I need a clinical diagnosis of what and why I was experiencing the symptoms that I was having. I must face the possibility that I may need to be readmitted to the hospital. I will not be happy, but it would undoubtedly provide me with the medical help I needed.

The patient advocate in me is coming to the surface. Currently, I am in the role of the patient advocate as the patient, and I have grown weary of what I feel is a great push-off. I have a ton of questions: What else can I expect during the recovery period? They will not be able to answer my questions, but I, as the patient, deserve an answer. Being provided with information is better than having no information at all.

Note to self: Call the PCP or file a formal grievance with the medical office administrator once this rash clears up to get the information, I need regarding how to reach the best health outcome possible without all the dips and gaps in my health status.

After eating, I sit down at my computer, but before logging into my insurance company's Provider Finder, I call my insurance company to inquire as to whether the information regarding the closure of medical providers and facility closings publicized by the media was true. It makes no sense for me to hunt to find an open medical office if they were all still closed. Success, the insurance customer service rep advises me that Urgent Care Center was open and providing medical services to patients. Using the insurance company's website, I quickly found an open location that was accepting walk-in appointments.

It was about ten 'o clock when I made it to the Center. After completing the COVID-19 assessment, I was triaged, and after waiting an additional thirty minutes, I was able to see the Nurse Practitioner. After my examination and the confirmed laboratory results, I was diagnosed with a yeast and bacterial infection. She advised me that both were common with the use of antibiotic medication. I was already aware of the relationship between antibiotics and yeast infections. Before COVID-19, I would have developed the yeast infection within a week after the completion of the medication. It took over a month for the symptoms to appear, and the aggressive way it did was not usual for me. A prescription for medication was called into my pharmacy.

On my way home from the Urgent Care Center, I stopped at the pharmacy to pick up the medication. Finally, I thought this would be all behind me, and I could gain peace of mind and begin to move forward. The notion of peace soon dissipated as I received another call from the pharmacy about an hour after reaching home. The call was to inform me that I had another prescription that was ready to be picked up. Confused about what additional medication needed to be picked up, I asked and was annoyed that my primary care doctor had ordered the same medicines called by the Nurse Practitioner. My primary doctor had blindly placed the order without examining me. I silently thought, how dare she order medication for me without first seeing me? The level of respect and the lack of distrust that was beginning to take shape in our patient-doctor relationship was raising red flags. This is her second time doing this. For a few hours, I let this thought bother me. I made a mental note to call her office or send a message through the patient portal to speak with her. I wanted to let her know that I was uncomfortable about her ordering medicine without taking the time to talk with me.

When an open line of communication exists between the patient and the provider, it presents a solution where everyone benefits from both. When the provider communicates well with the patient and has gained the patient's trust, the result is a partnership where the patient will be more apt to stay in compliance with the provider's guidance. When that communication line is either nonexistent or limited, the patient will often not follow the provider's guidance. An open line of communication between the patient-provider also shows that the provider welcomes input from the patient on how they feel their service needs should be met.

DIARY ENTRY: DAY 33

May 22, 2020. Who is that in the mirror? My body was unrecognizable when I woke up this morning. The only reason that I knew I was looking at myself was by the faraway look I held in my eyes and my hair scarf. The rest of my body resembled a big bottle of Ketchup. Red splotches were everywhere. The rash had spread a considerable amount. To say that I was a hot mess would be a major understatement. I was irritable to the point that I did not recognize my own thinking or actions. I knew I had to find relief, and I refused to sit around waiting for my primary care doctor to find time in her schedule to call me back. Self-help was once again high on my priority list.

Again, I called the 24/7 nurse line and advised them of what I was experiencing. I told them about my level of frustration in trying to reach my primary care doctor. The nurse apologized for the problems that I was having. She advised me that the pandemic was limiting the ability of doctors to be reached. She advised me to proceed to the Emergency Room or to Urgent Care. I opted to return to the Urgent Care office I had left the day before. Their office was closed, so I proceeded to the next closest clinic

Upon arriving at the new Urgent Care office,

my husband and I were greeted by a nursing team member in the parking lot. The nurse advised us that only the patient could enter the medical building due to the COVID-19 protocol and procedures that were in place. We advised him that I was the patient. He took a digital scan of my temperature, and when the reading showed I was without a fever, he directed me to where to go. Upon entering the office, the front desk receptionist gave me papers to complete and asked. "What is the nature of your visit?" I told her why I was there, and she advised me to take a seat and wait for my name to be called. I must have been sitting for about 15 minutes before a nurse called my name and asked me to step into the hall.

Once we were out in the hall, I was told that a medical doctor would not be able to see me that day. I was appalled and asked. "Why not?" The nurse stated that the rash could be a residual of COVID-19. This was without even looking at the rash to see what type it was. I left the building and phoned my husband to come to pick me up. My mind was beginning to race. Thoughts of worse-case scenarios related to future medical appointments were quickly filling my thinking space.

The reasoning behind why I was allowed to enter the building in the first place is a concept that has haunted my conscience since the incident happened. I should have been given an explanation the minute my husband and I pulled into the parking lot and encountered the nurse who took my vitals. We could have advocated then for my need to see a physician. The advocation may have been for nothing, but it would have been a learning experience. All it took was for the nurse to empathetically listen to my chief complaint. He could have then explained to me why I could not be treated there, and he could have also offered additional options on how or where to go to receive the medical services that were needed. Compassion was missing from the communication I had with the entire medical staff.

After reaching home, I called the insurance company and placed a complaint about how I was treated. I also asked for more options that were available to me for someone to look at the rash. Of course, the first option offered was for me to go to the Emergency Room. Another social issue that people in my community are unaware of is that the cost of seeking medical treatment in an Emergency Room versus a doctor's office is the excessive amount attached to the visit, another teachable moment. Emergency rooms always have a minimum of two bills attached. One is for the use of the facility, and the other is the physician's charge. Thus, unless it is a true emergency, one should avoid going to the Emergency Room. Not only that, but Emergency Room doctors have no patient history to guide their judgment on how to treat a patient. Since the rash was not life-threatening, I did not want to get stuck with paying high medical bills. I questioned the customer service representative at the insurance company on other options for medical treatment. They told me about an available telehealth service, and the price was the same as a traditional doctor's office visit. I opted to use the telehealth doctor. I was instructed to upload a photo of my rash into a portal accessible by the medical team. Moments later, I was connected to a medical doctor who advised me that the rash I had was not a residual of

COVID-19. A bacterial infection brought it on. I thought, WOW! It took him less than ten minutes to diagnose me. That sure was easy. That is all it would have taken had the doctor at the Urgent Care looked at the rash instead of rudely whisking me away due to the fear of the unknown. I was grateful that the doctor was able to provide me with a diagnosis and prescribe me medication. I was hopeful that the medicine would work and that I would restart the journey to one hundred percent healing. I soon found out that the hope I had would be short-lived.

I thought about how other people were wrongfully being denied treatment by medical providers, whether those people were told about alternative ways to receive care or whether the door was just being slammed in their faces. Such as what happened to me. Leaving people, especially those who are medically challenged, to try to fend for themselves only leads to problems for the patient and the community. Around this time, the media began reporting on an increase in the number of patients presenting with underlying conditions. After what I had just gone through, it was easy for me to un-

derstand why many patients do not proactively address their medical issues on their own. I
surmise that empathy in healthcare is missing.
We must get back to caring about each other
and ourselves.

CHAPTER 7

DON'T WAIT!

*Intelligent people are always
ready to learn. Their ears are
open for knowledge.*
-Proverbs 18:15 (NLT)

While I was growing up, I remember hearing my mother constantly telling me to always be prepared as I never knew when tough times would come. She would often tell me the importance of saving for a rainy day and never putting all my eggs into one basket. I have always held those words to be near and dear. I am very thankful that I followed her sage words of advice. Without these sage words, I am not sure I would have been able to manage all the twists and turns that my positive diagnosis of this virus had brought me.

This pandemic, as with prior pandemics, came unannounced. There was no sign or warning that it was coming. Future Pandemics will follow the same trajectory course. Thus, the urgency to prepare now for what lies ahead. One can no longer sit idly by and wait for devastation to occur.

The lessons I learned in dealing with this virus showed me the importance of being prepared for any type of emergency. These lessons were ones that I saw retroactively discussed on social media and in televised reports. I hope that sharing this information will help other people who have been diagnosed or the loved ones of those diagnosed with this virus or any other life-threatening illness heal without the anxiety and stress that often presents when it is least expected. Make no mistake about it : health-care challenges come as a puzzle; unless you are prepared to oversee them, they will cause undue pressure and add even more problems to your path of perfect healing.

Luckily for me, I have created a library of information. I refer to the resources contained within my library as my treasure trove. I refer to it quite often. I have continuously pulled information out of my library to deal with issues that have arisen. When I was building this trove, I never imagined it would be a lifesaver. Still, as I went through and used these tools daily, I silently thanked God for giving me the foresight to prepare for the unexpected.

I highly encourage everyone to review the checklist included in this book and create their list of must-haves. Then look at that checklist to ensure that you have all the things you need in the event of an unexpected health emergency. Remember: Once you have created and completed your own checklist of must-have items, tell your loved ones where it is kept.

Remember, life presents challenges that often come unexpectedly. My positive diagnosis of the Corona Virus was certainly not something I expected; however, such is life. My initiative-taking preparation for the unforeseen helped me tremendously. Be sure to talk to your loved ones about where to find the checklist should something unexpected occur. It should be readily available to your designated appointee.

Item #1 – Life Insurance.

A contract between an individual and a life insurance company, a.k.a. the insured and the insurer. The agreement is good for a period of usually 10-20 years or until the insured reaches 65 years old. The insured pays a recurring premium, a.k.a. payment on an agreed-upon date. In return, the insurer will pay the designated beneficiary a death benefit which is the value of the life insurance policy. If you are reading this book and do not have a life insurance policy. Please consider purchasing one and make sure that you keep your policy premium current. There are diverse types of Life Insurance policies. They include (*Be sure to seek the guidance of a professional life insurance broker. The information provided here is not intended as guidance or advice.*):

a. **Universal Life Insurance** - More commonly referred to as UL, is a form of permanent life insurance. There are two parts to a UL policy. UL policies offer an investment savings element and low premiums. The cost of a UL policy is the minimum amount of the policy premium. Beneficiaries receive the death benefit

b. Joint Life Insurance - There are two types of Joint life insurance policies. First, there is the first-to-die policy. This type of policy provides the surviving spouse with a death benefit after the loss of the spouse. The second Joint Life insurance policy pays a death benefit to the beneficiaries after the loss of both spouses.

c. Variable Life Insurance - A permanent life insurance policy with an investment part. Through the investment part of the policy, the insured has sub-accounts for which they can invest in. Variable life insurance policies come with a cash-value account.

d. Dependent Life Insurance - a voluntary life insurance program an employee is offered through their employer. This policy is often provided as a part of the benefits package provided by an employer.

e. Final (funeral/burial insurance) Expense Life Insurance - is a whole life insurance policy with a small death benefit and is easier to get approved for. Final expense is also referred to as simplified issue whole life insurance" or "modified whole life insurance

Item #2 -Supplemental Insurance Policy

Nothing spoke louder to me about the benefit of having supplemental insurance and its importance than the numerous reports publicizing the thousands of people losing their jobs and, in return, losing their health insurance. This is not a health insurance policy, but as a supplemental policy, it helps to minimize out-of-pocket costs by reimbursing for medical services that are often brought on by chronic illnesses. With a supplemental policy, an individual can concentrate more on getting better and less on worrying about paying bills.

There are several types of supplemental insurance policies. These types of policies can be purchased in a variety of ways. One way is through their employer group. They can also be purchased without the completion of a medical exam. There are limitations to supplemental insurance policies; therefore, before buying this type of policy, an individual must review it and, if necessary, speak with an insurance professional about the best type of policy to purchase. These types of policies are often purchased as an employee benefit. They end when you are no longer employed by the business. It is critically important for those who are employed to check to see if this is an employer-sponsored benefit. There will more than likely be a cost involved. Consider whether it is more advantageous to pay a few dollars per pay period now or risk having to pay thousands of dollars in the future for medical services. For those who are not employed, it is critically important that you immediately begin to investigate the purchase of an individual supplemental policy. Do not hesitate! It is imperative that this type of policy is added to your checklist. Remember, be prepared!

Item #3 – A Will

Nothing is more aggravating than losing a loved one and having squabbles regarding how to fairly divide the assets or private property of that loved one. A legally drafted and signed Will provides guidance on how to proceed with distribution after such a loss. It is important to remember that death often comes unannounced. Why leave your loved ones with the burden of arguing and fighting when you can take the time now to prepare? There are diverse types of Wills. They include:

a. **Living Will** - A legal document that tells others your personal choices about end-of-life medical treatment. It specifies the procedures or medications you prefer to prolong your life if you cannot speak to the doctors yourself.

b. **Last Will a.k.a. Last Will and Testament** - A legal document explaining exactly how a person wants their property and other assets to be managed after death. A Living Will indicates family responsibilities, i.e., naming legal guardians for minor children.

c. **Joint Will** - A legal document that two people sign together under most circumstances, a married couple. Instead of each spouse having their own will, the two parties agree on one joint document.

d. **Holographic Will**- A handwritten legal document drafted and signed by the person who is writing the will. The validity of this type of document is dependent upon the State Law where the person resides

e. **Nuncupative Will**- has little legal validity in most states in the United States. This type of Will can only be completed by a person who is in critical and facing imminent and immediate death.

f. **Deathbed Will** - A will that is written and signed by a person while they are on their deathbed

g. **Simple Will** - a basic will that lets a person draft an outline of how they want their stuff to be given away after their death. A basic will allows the person to specify whom they want to function as their representative

Item #4 -Trust

An essential legal documentation for property owners to have is a Trust, also referred to as a Revocable Living Trust. A binding agreement drafted and signed by the property owner provides information on who the named beneficiary is that the property will revert to upon the property owner's death. It is important to note that while Trusts are often thought of as a document for wealthy people, this is not the case. Trusts are for all property owners and are beneficial to have, so if a sudden death occurs, the property is distributed according to the requests stated in the binding document of a Trust.

If you are a property owner, remember that initiative-taking preparation is the key!

Item #5 -HIPAA

Health Information Affordability and Accountability Act (HIPPA) Paperwork As a trained healthcare professional, I have witnessed occasions where a patient's family has requested medical information for a loved one or family member. This request can be legally denied if documentation signed by the patient is not on file. Hesitation on your or your loved one's behalf to ensure that this documentation is on file can mean the difference between life and death. It can also mean the difference between receiving the correct medication or medicine that does not produce an allergic reaction that could cause detrimental harm. Remember, prepare now! Talk to your doctor, and make sure that the necessary paperwork is on file in their office. If not, make sure that you complete the paperwork. Encourage your loved ones to check with their medical providers to ensure that the necessary signed paperwork is on file. Take immediate action to implement this advice. The Health Insurance Portability and Accountability Act (HIPAA) disallows the sharing of information between medical providers and a patient's family. It is a law that cannot be circumvented. Without correctly completed and signed documentation, you will be unable to fulfill the following: (1) obtain healthcare information. (2) obtain an updated healthcare status, (3 have someone speak to medical providers on your behalf.

Act Now! Prepare Now! Sign that paperwork. You can thank me later.

Epilogue

MOVING FORWARD

*"At any given moment, you have
the power to say this is not
how my story is going to end."
– Unknown-*

According to published information, the length of time that one who was diagnosed with COVID-19 could exhibit symptoms of the virus was noted as ten to fourteen days. Yet, it was months later, and I was still sometimes reeling from the personal impact that the virus had on me. There were days that I still had memory issues, and my hormones left my body and mind chaotic. The eerie nightmares would sometimes appear, the rashes would keep coming one after the other, and my driving abilities diminished to the point where I would not drive for more than a block by myself for over a month. There were also days when my anxiety level was high, and I questioned my spirituality and belief in GOD. Yet, I persevered and kept pushing forward, uncertain of what the future had in store but confident that whatever came, I would be prepared to face the challenge.

I received a dozen or so email alerts from my social media accounts about friends and loved ones who had unfortunately lost their battle with the virus and had sadly passed away. I wondered how other people were finding themselves or their loved ones clinging to the hope that a cure would soon be found. The dismal days of dealing with the virus and the untimely deaths of their friends or loved ones seemed like they would never end. As a COVID-19 survivor and a Patient Advocate, I was intent on joining COVID-19 support groups. I wanted to assist as many people as possible in surviving and preparing for the upcoming challenges. I wanted to teach others how to use their voice to demand better and more healthcare resources, not just for this virus but for all the debilitating medical conditions that rock and dismantle the core of the communities that I belong to. I wanted to teach others, especially those living in what is referred to as the minority community, to become empowered patients and caregivers. I wanted to ensure that healthcare equity policies and procedures are written and policies are enacted into law.

I wanted to author a book that took my personal story and wove within it the intricacies of the healthcare system. So, I joined support groups and learned two valuable lifelong lessons. One of these lessons was that everyone had a personal story to share. A second lesson was that while each of us had been brought to the support group by an unknown source that had entered our lives or the life of our loved ones and placed on us unsurmountable moments and, at times, what seemed like a life-ending pain, we were determined not to give up. We were just as determined not to let others give up. We made it through the challenging times by coming together and sharing our difficulties, the highs and lows, and the memories of those we loved and lost. A third lesson I learned was how many people were affected by this dreadful disease. I was aware that many people had nowhere to turn and had mistakenly assumed that no one cared. I learned that some wanted and needed an empathetic ear. I learned that the world is full of warriors that believed they could and would beat this. I prayed and continued to pray that there will one day be a cure for this disease and all other diseases. The final lesson that I learned came to mind when I thought about the hardships of minority communities of color and women whenever a healthcare crisis arises.

I see a positive aspect in the future for those that are most often hardest hit with devastation. I smile, knowing that in my heart, I have prepared a blueprint that will prove to be extremely useful in moving forward the next time a Pandemic/Epidemic happens.

Corona Virus Necessity List

✖ <u>Self-Cleaning Products</u>
- Hand & Body Wipes
- Antiseptic Wipes
- Lotion/Moisturizers
- Facial Tissue
- Bath Soap
- Toothpaste
- Mouthwash
- Distilled Water

✖ <u>Household Products</u>
- Toilet Paper
- Paper Towels

✖ <u>Food & Water</u>
- Drinking water
- Fruits
- Yogurt
- Groceries

✖ <u>Misc.</u>
- Shipping

✖ <u>Cleansers/Disinfectant</u>

- Clorox or Store Brand Bleach
- Lysol
- Pine-Sol
- DIY (create your own disinfectant)

✖ <u>Medical Items</u>

- Medical Thermometer
- Finger Pulse Oximeter
- Rubbing Alcohol
- Tylenol-Fever Reducer
- Cold-Cough Medicine
- Pain Medicine
- Sterile Gloves
- Face Masks

✖ <u>Household Products</u>

- Toilet Paper
- Paper Towels

ABOUT THE AUTHOR

The debate regarding the topic of healthcare inequity is not new. Each time a Pandemic arises, the subject turns to the lack of healthcare resources for those living in minority communities. It is evident that a vested voice is needed to adequately address the problem of healthcare inequities and offer solutions that ensure that the discussion regarding healthcare inequities in minority communities moves from talk to action.

Sandra L. Washington has that vested voice. Her unquenchable thirst for "r ighting the wrongs" of healthcare inequity began over 25 years ago, after her son's birth, who was born with a heart condition that went unnoticed for the first three years of his life. She also experienced the harmful inequities in healthcare as she witnessed the challenges her very own sister faced while dealing with a rare heart condition. Wanting and determined to find solutions that will mitigate or even eliminate the inequities the black community faces.

The exacerbation of the lack of care Sandra's sister received from various clinicians, all of whom presumed a diagnosis without performing any testing. They instead based her diagnosis on her race, gender, and age, ultimately resulting in her death. Wrought with a broken heart from the experiences of her son and her sister, Sandra has written this book to shed light on the unspoken truths about healthcare inequities for black people, particularly older people. Sandra admits that she's "tired" of seeing older black people victimized by a healthcare system that minimizes the importance of testing for diagnosis. She has gotten way too comfortable issuing diagnoses based solely on demographics.

Sandra has a well-rounded perspective on the inequities of healthcare for older black people as she has spent over 30 years in the healthcare field, professionally and through her academic studies; she holds a Master of Public Policy Administration from Northwestern University. As a woman, a minority, a COVID-19 survivor, an "aged" individual, and a healthcare professional, Sandra has decided to use her distinctive voice to bring forth the need for significant change to bring equality in healthcare.

When she's not researching, writing, or speaking to others about the problems within the healthcare system and how to overcome those issues, Sandra spends her downtime listening to gospel music, spending time with her loving spouse, and encouraging her adult son. She also enjoys sharing her wisdom and encouragement with her family and friends. Sandra L. Washington was born and raised in New Jersey and now lives in Illinois with her husband.

ACKNOWLEDGEMENTS

First and foremost, I give honor to God for bringing me to and carrying me through the book writing process. Without his guidance this book would not have been written. While writing this book I experienced several health setbacks that often left me feeling drained and ready to quit. All I can say is, But God!

When I first started composing this book I knew or at least I thought I knew what information would be included in this book. I had a notebook filled with ideas on various ideas on what I was going to write and how I was going to write it. My goal was to write a story and make it clear about the healthcare challenges that I faced. It was me against the world. Little did I realize that what I saw unfolding for me was also unfolding for others. The healthcare inequities that I faced and the unequal access to healthcare resources that I was facing were obstacles for others as well. What I did not realize until I started drafting my book was that the issue of health inequities and unequal access is linked to the reason as to why it has been and continues to wreak havoc and bring alarmingly unsafe health conditions to minority communities.

There were numerous people who supported and encouraged me to complete this book. I will forever be thankful to my circle of friends and family that carried me through some very dark and painful days where I was ready to quit and sent an email or a text and told me that I could and would complete this book and that they would be first in line for their copy.

I owe a special debt of gratitude to the following people:

Vashti Redick Parks (Mom)- Thank you! Thank you! Thank you! for your constant prayers, your motherly love, your belief in your baby girl. You raised me to be a strong woman. A woman that stands up for what is right. A woman that stares systemic injustices squarely in the eye and not flinch but flight to overturn the wrongs and replace them with what is right.

Markus- My one and only child. You continuously show me that you believe in me and the hopes, dreams and goals that I have. You stepped in and stepped up whenever I asked. You put a smile on my face when you would remind me of just how far the two of us have come. Thank you for encouraging me to complete this book. From a mother's heart to a son's ears. I love you! Always have and always will!

L.C. – My dearest darling husband. My best friend. My partner for life. Thank you, a million times, for being the love of my life. From the first day that we met you have served as a prime example of what a friend, boyfriend, father, and husband should be. In addition to being an excellent role model for Markus you were /are my biggest cheerleader and supporter. When I want to give up you push me to see that quitting is not an option. You listened to me gripe and grumble and allowed me to take a short break but then you helped me get back up again and gave me a gentle nudge to get restarted again. My prayer is that our love continues to grow.

Endnotes

1 *Demographic Health Disparities and Health System Transformation: Drivers and Solutions, (November 2015) , Community Catalyst, from chrome-extension://efaidnbmnnnibpcajpcglclefindmkaj/https://www.communitycatalyst.org/wp-content/uploads/2022/11/Policy-Brief-Demographic-Health-Disparities-Final.pdf?1447360066*

2 *The National Coordinating Council for Medication Error Reporting and Prevention3 (Tariq & Scherbak, 2021), from https://www.nccmerp.org/about-medication-errors*

www.ingramcontent.com/pod-product-compliance
Lightning Source LLC
Chambersburg PA
CBHW022053050726
47591CB00002B/514